The Mind-Made Prison

Mateo Tabatabai

Revised Edition

Copyright

Table of Contents

CHAPTER 1
The Mind-Made Prison

Once you start to awaken from the mind-made prison, you will inevitably wonder whether you have gone insane or whether you have just started to see how crazy your interpretations of the world have always been. It is a deeply surreal thing to realize that you have been living in a huge illusion, and it is fascinating how quickly you forget that you were once asleep.

I was 6 years old when I first realized that something just wasn't right. I couldn't yet put words to what it was that I felt; I just had this inner knowing that I never wanted to live life like everyone else did when I grew up. Life for grown-ups seemed so serious, and unlike most other children, I was in no hurry to grow up and become an adult.

As I became older, I slowly forgot about the insight I had when I was 6 years old. I jumped right into the mind-made prison just like most other people do. I started believing that my worth as a human being was based on my achievements, that people had to like me, and that life was unfair. Of course, I didn't realize that I actually believed these things until much later.

I was so caught in the mind-made prison that I no longer understood I was a prisoner. It took some dramatic events for me to wake up to my true nature again and remember the vow I had taken when I was just 6 years old. I once again remembered that a life of captivity and suffering was not an option for me.

As I am writing this, I am sitting on a balcony on the second story and watching the Mediterranean Sea. Right now it has a beautiful turquoise color to it, and as the sun casts its reflection on the still water, I take a deep breath and look at the palm trees between the sea and me.

My feet are resting on the edge of the balcony, and for a moment, I become aware of how relaxing it is to just let them surrender to gravity while the heat of the sun gently caresses them.

There is a young shepherd dog sleeping in the grass beneath the balcony, and as I look to my left, I notice a cat suddenly waking up, alerted by the sound of hammering in the distance. I take another deep breath and thank the divine source that I am here in this place. I not only thank Him for where I am physically, I also thank Him for the perspective from which I am viewing this moment.

Today I realize that the question is not whether we are caught in the mind-made prison. The real question is to what degree are we prisoners of our own minds? We are all living in an illusion and mistaking it for reality.

This illusion is the cause of all your suffering in life. Not just some or even the majority of your suffering; it is the sole cause of all the accumulated suffering you have experienced since your first memory and up to this present moment.

I know you think you have free will and that you are a conscious being acting exactly the way you want to act. I understand that you think you are logical and only go for the things you really want. I know this, and still I am here to tell you that what you perceive as free will is nothing but an illusion designed to cover up the fact that you are constantly reacting to whatever happens. What you perceive as conscious choice is nothing but an automatic response.

As you are reading this you are reacting to it in a certain way without being aware of why you are doing so. You might be feeling frustrated, curious, or shocked, or perhaps you put this book aside because you don't like it.

Your suffering doesn't come from having an opinion; the suffering comes from not realizing that you are interpreting everything you experience. One of the signs of being a prisoner of the mind is constantly having to label things and determine whether they are true or not.

We have all these "true" stories about who we are, what we can achieve, how our life is, how the world is, and how people treat us. We have all these stories and yet we have no idea that we are prisoners of our own minds. We are constantly mistaking our subjective interpretations of the world as truth, and it is causing us immense suffering.

We are so sure about who we are that we get offended when someone questions it. We are so sure about our beliefs that we defend them and have arguments over them. We are so sure of the correct way to live life that we look down on others who live differently.

We like the people who support our beliefs and dislike the ones who don't. If people don't like our appearance, we resent them. We seek and defend the truth because we think such a thing really exists! We argue, get depressed, fight, and kill for the truth!

You want to know why we don't have peace here on Earth? Because of people who "know" the truth and want to shove their reality down the others' throats.

It is time to put down your weapon and shield because what you are trying to defend is not really the truth. No concept, theory, or word can ever contain the whole truth. Everything is, and always will be, relative.

> "Everything we hear is an opinion, not a fact. Everything we see is a perspective, not the truth."
>
> —Marcus Aurelius

I understand that you might feel you know the truth and that I am just the idiot claiming to know better. But what if you just let go of your knowing for a short while? What if you could forget everything you know to be true about yourself and started exploring parts of you that you had never explored before?

You don't explore what you already know, and most people think they know everything about themselves. Since you are reading this book, there must be something you want to improve in your life. The only way you can find what you are looking for is to stop knowing so much.

- When was the last time your mind wasn't controlling you?

- When was the last time you just listened to someone instead of thinking about what you were going to reply or whether or not they were right?

- When was the last time you did what you truly wanted to, without letting what others thought of you affect you?

I want you to come back to these three questions after reading this book and answer them again.

When you realize that everything is just a perspective, you become free for the first time in your life. It gives you peace and removes the burden of having to act according to who you "are." It removes the burden of having to constantly defend what you believe, and you no longer have to get defensive when someone doesn't agree with your perspective. I know your perspective on life seems so real, but it is simply made up by your imagination.

Soon you will see that there is no good or bad, only an interpretation of what is. You will realize that your whole experience is based solely on your interpretation of external events that are completely neutral. You will understand that you have nothing figured out and that all the things you thought you knew are only imaginary constructs of your mind. You have so much talent and potential inside you that is not coming through because your mind has imprisoned you.

You have an incredible opportunity here, and it is up to you to let go of your existing truths in order to seize it. Empty your cup and become free, or continue what you have been doing and see where it takes you.

The Ultimate Consequence of the Mind-Made Prison

You are lying on your deathbed, and you know that you are going to leave this wonderful place soon. You have had many experiences in life, but what keeps popping up in your mind are all the things you didn't do.

Somehow, your failures and times of being ridiculed really don't matter that much anymore, and you think more about your true successes, your deep moments of love, your passions, and your times of letting go and flowing with life.

You smell the lavender incense by your bed and take a trip down memory lane to the first love of your life. You remember this person in great detail, and this memory brings a big smile to your face.

Suddenly, a nagging feeling interrupts this beautiful moment. At first it is a feeling of not being comfortable, but it quickly starts building and turns into a deeply rooted pain. You feel the pain in your chest and stomach, but it is like no physical or emotional pain you have ever felt.

You wonder to yourself whether this is what physical death feels like, a thought that you quickly dismiss because you know you are still alive.

You suddenly see shadows standing around your deathbed. These shadows don't look evil, and it just seems like they have a message for you. This calms you down a bit, and you become curious about what they have to say.

However, their expressions slowly start changing, and you begin to feel uneasy again when you see their condemning eyes. You start panicking, and your whole life flashes before your eyes in what seems to be just a couple of seconds.

They are still not saying anything, the energy in the room starts to get gloomy, and you have an icy feeling in your bones.

This feels nothing like what you had imagined your last moments on Earth would be like. You are now so caught up in the meaning of these shadows that you forget that most of your family is still with you in the room.

All you can focus on are these shadows, and you see that they look jaded and disappointed. You get mad at them for ruining your last moments on Earth and you yell, "What do you want??? Leave me alone!!"

After a long pause, one of the shadows finally speaks up and asks You, "Why? Why did you just squander us when we were always ready to serve you?" The shadows start crying, and you can see that they are absolutely heartbroken. Their tears are so heartfelt that even you are affected.

You ask them who they are.

Everything gets completely quiet for what seems to be an eternity, and they finally reply, "We are your talents, abilities, and unlimited potential. We were always here for you, but now we are going to leave Earth forever, and we never got a chance to make a difference. Not because you or we couldn't, but because you never allowed yourself to embrace your true light."

The saddest tear you have ever felt in your life runs down your cheek and your eyes close. Your last thought before leaving Earth is, "If only I could have another chance."

My dear friend, you have been asleep. Most of humanity has been asleep, but we are waking up. One by one we are waking up and we are shaking life into everyone who is still a prisoner of their mind. I invite you to wake up and join the rest of us in the experience of heaven on Earth.

When you are no longer a captive of your mind, you can be, do, or have anything. It is time to wake up and realize this.

CHAPTER 2
This Is Who You Are

Who Are We?

We are creators of our own experience. We are expert creators who are constantly shaping, molding, and creating meaning. One of the great tragedies in life is that most people never truly get to realize the sheer power and potential of this innate ability.

It is not wrong to create meanings and representations of things; in fact, it is our very nature to do so. You are going to interpret the world whether you like it or not. You are never truly seeing "reality" exactly as it is, even when you are absolutely sure of something.

If there is any one skill in life that could give you infinite happiness, wealth, connection, and self-esteem, it is your ability to create meaning.

Whether I write **meaning, thought, interpretation, representation, rules**, or **belief** in this book, I am always referring to the same thing; don't get confused by the terminology.

Life is an internal experience mistaken for an external one. You never truly see what is going on in the external world; all you are seeing is the interpretation you choose to give an external event. There is no such thing as a negative or positive external event. Whether something is negative or positive depends solely on the meaning you are creating and how you choose to represent an external experience in your mind.

For those who grow up in a Western culture, people who eat dog meat seem evil or twisted in some way. We don't have to look any further than the early 20th century, however, to find that dog meat was sold in butcher shops and consumed during times of food shortage in the United States.

In Germany, dog meat was eaten until the 1920s, in the Netherlands dog meat sausages were common up to the 1940s, and as you may know, it is still pretty common in some Asian countries. The only reason we think something is negative or positive is because of the internal interpretations we make.

At the time I write this, a new law has just been signed in the United States that makes it legal to slaughter horses for consumption.. This means that it is now legal to kill and consume horses! Wouldn't you think it was weird if you heard of some "barbaric" country where it was legal to kill horses and eat them?

Well, a lot of slaughterhouse owners are ecstatic about this new law, and many animal activists are absolutely shattered. It all depends on the perspective!

I want you to remember a scenario where someone insulted you and really got to you. Really remember what they said word for word. Feel the emotions you felt when it happened. It really got to you when this person insulted you, didn't it?

What if a 3-year-old child came up to you and said the exact same thing and really tried his or her hardest to insult you? Chances are that you would react in a completely different way and in most cases, you would forget about it pretty quickly.

The only difference between these two scenarios is the interpretation you make about the external world. In the first scenario, you probably feel that what that person did was wrong, you were treated unfairly, you were humiliated, you seemed weak, you felt helpless, etc. In the second scenario, most people would just brush it off and say, "He's just a kid, he doesn't know what he's talking about" or "Wow, he's a cheeky little one, isn't he?"

Most people understand this on some level, but still they think this power is somehow dependent on external events. They can create positive meanings when a child offends them. However, it is impossible to do so when your boss, spouse, or parents do the same thing.

They don't realize their interpretation is just another meaning they have created in their mind and that it is holding them back from complete and utter freedom. They could have just as well created the interpretation that it is extremely easy to have control over ANY meaning they choose to create. If your mind is trying to determine whether this is true or not, you are not getting my point.

I can't prove to you whether a meaning or belief is true or false, but I definitely know which meanings are going to be the most constructive and helpful in living a high-quality life. If you feel that you have a low quality of life right now, it simply means that you have been creating low-quality meanings. How skillful you are at creating meanings that empower you, is going to determine the quality of your life.

Do you understand how powerful it is to realize this? To truly understand that meaning doesn't exist OUT THERE and that you have the innate ability to represent something external any way you like in your mind?

This isn't even a skill you have to learn, since you are already doing it every second of your life without giving it a thought. We will get more into this skill in the later chapters. By the end of this book you are going to have a firm grasp of how you can use this ability to greatly improve the quality of your life.

The best thing about your ability to create meanings is that you don't have to wait until you reach hundreds of goals in the future before you can allow the quality of your life to improve. You can do it right NOW, simply by creating different meanings.

Before we move on, I want to look at some of the created meanings and beliefs that can hold you back when it comes to growing and becoming free in your life. Don't beat yourself up if you operate with any of these beliefs. Just recognize that they are there and keep an eye on how they affect your view of the things I am going to share with you throughout this book.

These are some of the meanings and beliefs that can hold you back from reclaiming your power as the creator of your life experience:

- If I am happy and content with my life right now, I will lose all motivation to reach any of my future goals.

- Change might be easy for some people, but I am not someone who can welcome change easily.

- Controlling the meanings I create will make me inconsiderate towards others.

- If I am too happy, I will seem like a maniac to others.

- Positive thinking means that I pretend things are good when they are not. If I became really positive I wouldn't be able to fix all of the things that need fixing because I would deceive myself into thinking everything was fine.

- People who are optimistic are not realistic at all.

- I need x and y in order to be happy and I won't trick myself into feeling happy emotions before I have them.

- If I take control of my mind, I will become just like a robot.

- If I suddenly start changing too much, people will dislike me and think I am a weird self-development fanatic.

- I have responsibilities to take care of; I don't have time for luxuries like complete happiness or self-improvement.

These are just some of the beliefs that can hold you back when it comes to reclaiming your power. There are also many more beliefs that can stop you dead in your tracks. Because I believe that you know yourself better than anyone else ever will, I want you to think about some other beliefs you might have that could hinder your learning and development.

The next thing I want you to do is to define the concept of the Unknown and see what it means to you. Each person has their own associations and meanings to given words, and when it comes to growth and change, it is very important to take a look at your associations to the concept of the Unknown.

An example of this:

My current associations to the Unknown: Excitement, growth, energy, courage, being ready for whatever, empowerment, and knowing that I am growing because I am not afraid of getting out of my comfort zone.

My associations to the Unknown 6 years ago: Fear, risk, failure, possibly being judged, uncomfortable, not necessary, and dangerous.

How likely is it that you are going to be willing to develop and change your ways if you have a negative association to the concept of the Unknown?

Transformation Exercise

Become aware of the associations you currently have to the Unknown. After you have found them, I want you to take a look at what other meanings you could use that would make it easier for you to move into the Unknown and seize the opportunity to grow.

Here is a list of some meanings you could add to your definition of the Unknown (I won't charge you extra, so use as many as you like): Success, growth, determination, spirit of the champion, warrior mentality, elite performance, happiness, exhilaration, acceptance, vitality, power, movement, velocity, invincibility, greatness, accomplishment, victory, evolution, fortitude, vigor, tenacity, ecstasy, delight, flexibility, flow.

Looking at your associations to the Unknown is just a tiny example of the power of meaning and how it can either propel you forward or hold you back. If you have negative associations to the Unknown, you are going to do everything in your power to stay away from situations where you don't have absolute control.

This includes approaching your soul mate if you are lucky enough to suddenly spot him or her in the street, starting the business you have always dreamed of, growing as a person; basically anything where you perceive the "unknown" factor to be too great.

Change your meaning of the Unknown and suddenly the same external situation is completely different. Isn't it weird that your view of just one concept such as the Unknown can make a huge difference to what you do and experience in life?

Most people's life quality can be drastically improved by just finding 5 to 10 of their limiting beliefs and changing them. Each one of your beliefs has the power to create either depression or joy in your life.

The kicker is that you have thousands and thousands of beliefs that you are not even aware of, and while some of them are helping you, I am willing to bet that there are also a couple in there that are giving you negative emotions. In fact, the average person will have many beliefs that are directly detrimental to their level of happiness.

In order to fully understand the impact your beliefs have on your life, we first have to understand the underlying mechanisms of beliefs. I have simplified the theory part of this chapter as much as I can, and I have only included the theory we are actually going to use to create changes in your life. If you don't understand everything the first time around, it is no big deal, just continue reading and you will get it before long.

What Are Beliefs?

Meaning is a thought, opinion, interpretation, representation, or belief about something or someone.

Examples of meanings/beliefs

- Eating unhealthy foods will make you fat (a belief about unhealthy foods).

- You have to work hard in order to make money (a belief about acquiring money).

- My mom is a nice person (a belief about your mom).

These are all "single" beliefs, but you only believe them because there are other beliefs that are supporting them. For example, the belief that your mom is a nice person is also a meta-belief.

Meta is the Latin word for higher, and a meta-belief is a "higher" understanding of all of your collected beliefs in a given area of life. You have meta-beliefs for every single area of your life. Some examples are your meta-beliefs for money, health, relationships, sex, and communication. A meta-belief can consist of tens, hundreds, or even thousands of different beliefs you have created throughout your life.

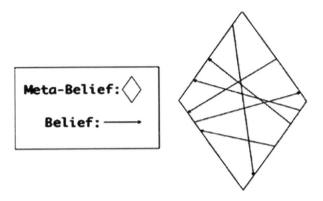

Let's take a look at some meta-beliefs and see what types of beliefs they can be constructed from.

Meta-belief (higher understanding of underlying beliefs):

- By competing with others and putting them down, I become a more valuable person.

Beliefs (underlying beliefs that led to the higher understanding):

- Life is about proving that you are the best.

- My value as a human being lies in what I do and how others perceive me.

- It's a dog-eat-dog world out there.

- If someone is doing something stupid, they are asking to be put down.

- If someone is doing well in life, it means they are taking away from me.

21

- People are out to get me and I have to get them first.

- You can only trust your family and very close friends; you should keep your distance from other people.

- Gossip is normal and everyone does it.

- If there is any truth to what you are saying, it is completely okay to put others down.

- Either you win or you lose.

- The limelight is limited, and there is not enough room for two people.

As you can see, this meta-belief is primarily related to the arenas of success, self-worth, competition, and image.

Meta-belief (higher understanding of underlying beliefs):

- You can only be a good person by constantly giving to others.

Beliefs (underlying beliefs that led to the higher understanding):

- Taking care of yourself is being conceited. Nobody likes a selfish person.

- You are not loved for who you are, but for what you do for others.

- If I don't sacrifice myself for others, I will be judged and people will criticize me.

- Nobody wants to spend time with someone who is selfish.

- Only people who give to others are worth anything.

- A giving person goes to heaven.

- People always accept and validate me when I sacrifice myself in order to please their needs.

- If others do not validate me, I am not a worthy person.

- You can't receive without immediately giving back.

- I have to give something to others before I feel worthy of receiving.

- All people have to like me and see me as a nice person.

This meta-belief is primarily connected to the arenas of relationships, self-worth, and image.

Meta-Belief (higher understanding of underlying beliefs):

- In life, you are judged by your accomplishments.

Beliefs (underlying beliefs that led to the higher understanding):

- How successful I am in life determines my worth.

- If you don't have an education, you are stupid.

- Being successful in life gives you passion and joy.

- Poor people are full of excuses and don't take responsibility for their lives.

- People who value things like love, spirituality, and religion, usually do so because they can't accomplish anything else.

- Women love wealthy men.

- Enough success will eventually give you happiness.

- Only measurable things like education level, wealth, property, and cars really count in life.

- All successful people are living the life of their dreams.

- If you are successful, everyone will accept and validate you.

- You can only be respected by being successful.

- If you are not successful, people of higher status will walk all over you.

This meta-belief is primarily dealing with respect, image, success, and people.

Meta-Belief = Belief

You might already have realized that each underlying belief is in fact a Meta-Belief of its own (it consists of even more underlying beliefs).

This means that all beliefs are in fact both meta-beliefs and underlying beliefs at the same time. They are meta-beliefs because they offer a higher understanding of a lot of underlying beliefs. They are underlying beliefs because they cluster with other Beliefs to create and support another meta-belief.

An easy way to show this is to use the belief "My mom is a nice person."

Meta-belief:

- My mom is a nice person.

Some underlying beliefs that make this belief true for you:

- My mom is a nice person because she is caring.

- My mom is a nice person because she always supports me.

- My mom is a nice person because she checks up on me when I am sick.

In this case all of your underlying beliefs are clustering together to create the meta-belief (higher understanding) that your mom is a nice person. This same meta-belief could also cluster with other underlying beliefs in order to create another meta-belief.

Meta-belief:

- I love my Mom.

Underlying beliefs that make this belief true to you:

- I love my mom because she gave birth to me.

- I love my mom because she took care of me when I was a baby.

- I love my mom because she is a nice person.

Let me give you another example where I go down the "levels" of a given belief. In this example I will continue exploring the underlying beliefs of every single belief that we find.

Meta-belief:

- You can only be a good person by constantly giving to others.

One of the underlying beliefs/meta-beliefs:

• You are not loved for who you are, but for what you do for others.

One of the underlying beliefs/meta-beliefs:

• People will only appreciate you if you give them things; for example, help, service, support, or compliments and if you sacrifice yourself for them.

One of the underlying beliefs/meta-beliefs:

• By doing something for someone else you can show them the qualities you have and why you should be appreciated.

One of the underlying beliefs/meta-beliefs:

• I only have permission to validate myself as being good enough if I first get the validation of someone else after doing something for him or her.

One of the underlying beliefs/meta-beliefs:

• I am not worthy enough to tell myself I am good enough.

One of the underlying beliefs/meta-beliefs:

• I don't have the qualities needed to tell myself I am good enough right now.

Some of the underlying beliefs/meta-beliefs:

• I am not confident.

• I fear too many things.

- I am unlucky.

- I just don't get things the first time.

- Other people have a much easier life than I do.

In this last example, I included a couple of the underlying beliefs just to show you that we can continue going down in each belief/meta-belief for as long as we want and eventually we will cross paths with a belief we have already been through.

In reality this is what your operating system looks like:

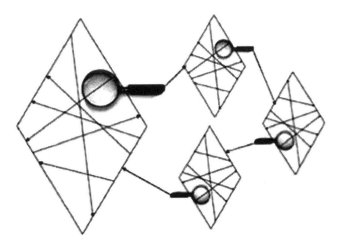

This figure is a representation of how a meta-belief consists of several underlying beliefs and how each of these underlying beliefs is a meta-belief in and of itself when you start exploring it.

As you can see, meta-beliefs/beliefs are complex structures of the mind that are built and reinforced by other beliefs/meta-beliefs.

All of your beliefs are connected to each other, either directly or indirectly, and each belief functions as an "underlying support" for why another belief is true. This means that if you have just a couple of limiting beliefs, those beliefs can cluster together to create tens or hundreds of new limiting beliefs. Of course, the same mechanism is true for positive beliefs.

We will get to the bottom of this phenomenon later, when we explore how we are constantly reinforcing and finding additional evidence for our existing beliefs.

I explain the interconnectedness of your beliefs because it will help us when it comes to creating changes. Because our beliefs are all connected as a part of a bigger picture and they are all affecting each other, we don't need to examine every single belief we have.

We can simply find the beliefs that are having a huge effect on a lot of our other beliefs and create shifts where it really matters. We find these beliefs through self-inquiry and asking questions that will allow us to go "down" in levels until we find a belief that has a big effect on our other beliefs.

Let's use as an example one of the beliefs we discussed earlier in this chapter: "By doing something for someone else, you can show them the qualities you have and why you should be appreciated." It is easy to see that changing that belief to a more positive one will probably make a big difference in your life.

By going deeper, however, we found an even richer belief that had a lot more control over our behaviors in "I am not worthy enough to tell myself I am good enough." This belief is a much bigger leverage point than the first one. If you change it to a more positive one, you are going to have large shifts all across the board because of the natural interconnectedness of our beliefs.

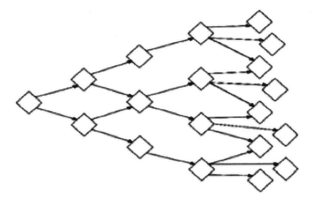

**A belief that functions as a leverage point and creates
large shifts in your other beliefs.**

I want to make it very clear that beliefs are not right or wrong, good or bad. The only question I care about is whether the beliefs that are running your life are improving or decreasing its quality.

This means that whenever I refer to a belief as negative or positive in this book, I am only talking about whether or not it is improving the quality of your life. Now that you understand that all beliefs are also meta-beliefs and vice versa, I will just use the word belief from now on, in order to make things as simple as possible.

The Model

I work with a model of behavior that is very simple to understand:

Belief --» Reaction + Justification

This simple model determines how you are constantly reacting in your life. The first step towards free will is to understand the underlying principles.

Belief: An understanding about a given area of life or a situation.

29

Reaction: How you "choose" to react in different circumstances and to different experiences in life. Your reactions are completely determined by the kind of beliefs you have running in the background.

Justification: This is the story you build around a given reaction, and your justification explains why you did what you did. In 9 of 10 cases your justifications are NOT the real reason you reacted as you did, your beliefs are.

Let's look at some practical examples of how this model works in relation to your limiting beliefs, so that we don't get too caught up in the theory. In the table below I have written the reaction and justification first and the belief that is their root last. This is how people typically perceive and experience things in life, but in reality it is the belief that is causing you to react to and justify things in a certain way.

Reaction	Justification	Belief (that caused the reaction and justification)
You act arrogant to keep people away.	People just don't get me, most of them are stupid and I can't relate to them.	Connecting with people means that you risk getting hurt.
You are afraid to ask people for what you want or state your opinion	I am a nice person and it would be intrusive to state my opinion.	Expressing yourself means risking rejection.
You reject every single idea someone presents to you.	That was a really stupid idea. It takes so much effort going through with that idea that it is not worth the time.	Stepping into the unknown is dangerous and often leads to failure.
You walk around with your shoulders and neck all tense, hide your emotions and constantly try to show everyone how tough you are.	I am always ready and I can see right through people.	If people think I am naïve, they will take advantage of me.
You gossip about others and criticize them.	If I don't talk about them someone else will.	By competing with others and putting them down, I become a more valuable person.
You call a woman a slut because she sleeps with someone.	I am a guy who has self-respect and I hate it when I see women who don't respect themselves.	The core of all men is to take advantage of men and if you allow them to get too close, they will ruin your life.
You offend homosexual people and tell them they are sinners.	I am only doing it for their own good because I don't want them to go to hell when they die.	What I don't understand is dangerous and a potential threat to me.

Continued on next page . . .

You get in a fight with someone who flirts with your girlfriend.	*It is his own fault; he should have never disrespected my honor.*	If I don't protect my girlfriend's honor she will think I am weak and stop loving me.
When someone yells at you, you yell back and continue to escalate the altercation.	*I had to show him who is the boss or else he would step all over me.*	If I get humiliated in front of others, it means that I lose my worth as a human being.
You are extremely giving and sacrifice yourself for others.	*I am a really good person and giving just comes naturally.*	You can only be a good person by constantly giving to others.
You constantly overeat and procrastinate on taking care of your body.	*You can't be on a diet all the time, some times you just need to relax.*	Skinny and athletic people are fanatics who don't have any freedom and they also tend to be stuck-up.
You are a womanizer who seduces and charms every woman you meet.	*I just can't hold myself back when I see a woman.*	I am only good enough if women accept me.
You don't ask out the guy you really like.	*I think he already has a girlfriend and besides, it would seem pretty desperate to just go up and ask him out.*	If someone rejects me it means that I am not a desirable person.

You think you are in control, but in reality your beliefs are controlling everything. This isn't problematic in and of itself, because no matter what you do, your beliefs are always going to be in control.

If we couldn't rely on our beliefs as a means of operating in daily life, we would never evolve or grow, because we would constantly have to learn the same thing over and over again. But how are we going to become the master of our experience if our beliefs are always going to be in control? We are going to do so by **choosing** the beliefs we want to operate with.

Just because you don't have control over the content of a CD once you put it in the computer, that doesn't mean that you can't just take out that CD and insert a different one instead.

We have what I refer to as psychological blind spots. A blind spot is a thought, belief, or value that has become such an integral part of our identity that we no longer see it or the pain that it is causing us. Because most people are not aware of the beliefs that are running everything, it seems as though their justifications are really the genuine reason for why they do things.

They really believe the illusion of their justifications and accept them as truth. Not only do they accept their justifications as the ultimate truth, they are also willing to defend them if someone challenges them.

If I went up to somebody and started pointing out their limiting beliefs and explained to them that their justifications are not really true, they are very likely to become defensive and try to defend their stories for why they do things.

This isn't necessarily because they are closed-minded or not willing to change. It is simply because their justifications are serving a purpose. It is my belief that our mind is doing its best to look out for us and that we only do things because we believe that it is ultimately what is going to serve us best.

This means that even though some of your beliefs are causing you immense pain in your life, they continue to run because your mind perceives them to have some sort of protective function. This is why your mind constructs justifications so that they seem completely real to you. The mind understands that if you accept the justification as reality, you won't dig around and attempt to find the real reason behind your reaction.

As a result, you won't find the belief that got you to react to begin with. In this way the protective belief survives and continues "serving" you. A lot of times even the beliefs that now seem negative actually used to serve a purpose for you.

For example, having the belief that "I should keep people at a distance because you can't trust people" might have been appropriate if you grew up in a situation where trusting the wrong person could have meant a threat to your survival.

The belief that "I shouldn't get intimate with people because it means I can get hurt" might have really helped you at a time when you had just been hurt and you really couldn't handle getting your heart broken again.

The challenge occurs when you don't look at your beliefs and question whether they are still serving you or not. When you carry around beliefs and interpretations about the world that are no longer serving you, you start suffering.

A belief is not bad in and of itself; it is the context of the belief that determines whether it is serving you or not. Keeping people at a certain distance might be a good idea growing up in a dangerous environment, but if you continue doing that once you go to college, you are not going to have a lot of fun.

Let's look at an example of how this pattern functions in real life. Let's say one of your beliefs is that you are afraid of being intimate with people because of the possibility of getting hurt. Your reaction to this belief is that you will find a reason to bring things to a halt every time you really start connecting with someone. You consequently justify this behavior by saying you are not really ready for a relationship yet and you just want to have fun. Because the justification created by your mind is engineered in a cunning way, you will believe that it is true. Believing the justification will keep you from finding the real reason for why you push people away when they get too close. In this way your mind has kept you from looking deeper and becoming aware of the fact that you are afraid of getting hurt and its job is complete.

Your belief that "intimacy = risk of getting hurt" protects you because it keeps you from connecting too deeply with people and as a result, no one can ever hurt you. You might even feel really lonely and depressed about the fact that you can never meet anyone on a conscious level.

On a subconscious level, however, you are getting the benefit of never allowing anyone to hurt you. This phenomenon is called the secondary benefit. A secondary benefit simply means that even though something is causing you pain on one level, it is giving you a greater level of pleasure on another level.

If your mind doesn't give you a really clever justification that you will completely believe and view as the truth, you might find the belief that is running in the background. If you found this belief, you might come to the conclusion that it was stupid and start allowing yourself to connect deeply with others.

Now you might really enjoy this, but your mind will not. From your Mind's perspective, this puts you at risk, and therefore it doesn't want you to find the "protective" belief running in the background. This can sound contradictory to what I said earlier about how your mind only wants what is best for you, but the explanation is actually quite simple: Your mind completely believes whatever meanings you have created.

Because it views your beliefs as truth, it will view getting hurt as a very frightening experience and it will do anything in its power to keep you from taking such a risk. If, instead, you had the belief that "getting hurt is a risk you have to run if you ever want to feel love," your mind would no longer view getting hurt in as negative a light, and as a result, it wouldn't find it necessary to "protect" you from getting hurt.

You have decided what your mind feels it needs to protect you from by the beliefs you have chosen to believe in. If you believe that failure and public embarrassment are the worst things that can happen in life, your mind is going to feed you all kinds of stories and justifications for why you shouldn't go ahead and follow your dreams.

By doing this, your mind is in fact serving its purpose by protecting you from failure and public embarrassment. It is only doing this because YOU have given it the instruction that failure is something that should be avoided at all cost.

If you saw failure as a completely natural part of life and believed that the fastest way to become successful is to get out of your comfort-zone and double your rate of failure, your mind would react very differently. It would even start giving you stories and justifications for why you need to fail more, so you can get more reference points and ultimately succeed faster.

You are always going to justify what you do and build stories around a given event. While some people can justify eating another pizza even though they are severely overweight, others will justify getting less sleep in order to reach their goals faster.

From the outsider's perspective, you might say that it is actually a good idea to sleep less in order to reach your goals faster and that there is no point in looking for the belief that underlies this justification. I agree that for some people this might work, but for others the health sacrifice would simply be too big to warrant it.

If your number one value in life is your health, it is not going to improve the quality of your life to believe that it is okay to deprive yourself of sleep in order to reach your goals faster. If your number one value in life is success, however, you might feel that this belief is actually improving your life.

I am going to repeat this point again: There is no right or wrong belief. The only thing that matters is whether or not a belief is improving the quality of your life or not. You need to be brutally honest when you look at your beliefs and see whether they are giving you positive and joyous emotions in the long run.

Your mind will accept ANY belief you decide to adopt, and even if there is not an ounce of truth to your belief, you will start believing it with enough programming and repetition. Your mind is always trying to do what's best for you, and it uses the beliefs you have chosen to adopt as a way of determining which direction is "best" for you.

Let's look into another example from my own life. Ever since I was a child I had a passion for writing, and I even tried writing a fantasy book when I was 11 years old. As I grew older, I traveled the world and trained with some of the best teachers in different fields of self-improvement and spirituality.

This gave me a lot of valuable insights, and at the age of 18, I started coaching others while continuing my own education and progress.

After having trained hundreds of people who all got impressive results in their lives, I had no doubt that I had the skills and talent to help not only myself, but also others. As I continued my travels and education, I became even better at understanding people, but I still hadn't written my first book.

My justification for not putting my thoughts down in writing was that I wanted my first book to be perfect and in order to reach this goal, I needed to learn even more things. This justification seemed completely natural to me, and I really thought that it was true. The more I believed this story, the more I procrastinated on writing my book and reaching an even bigger audience.

You have to remember that writing a book wasn't just some idea that had popped up in my mind in order to make more money or become famous. It was something I had wanted to do ever since I was 11 years old and it was literally one of my childhood dreams. This just goes to show that our justifications can seem so true that they will hold us back from following up on our deepest childhood desires.

I finally found the belief that was holding me back and making me procrastinate: "If I don't have massive success with my first book, it means that I have failed." Because I perceived myself to be extremely good at helping people, my mind didn't want me to risk ruining that picture by writing a book that didn't live up to my own perceived skills (secondary benefit).

Bear in mind that at this point I had been a public speaker for a couple of years and I had no problem speaking in front of hundreds of people. I had put myself on the line hundreds of times by taking on challenging clients and risking failure.

See, logically I knew that it was a great idea to write a book. I knew that it would motivate me to work even harder towards becoming a world-renowned transformations coach. However, because I had the belief that "If I don't have massive success with my first book it means that I have failed," my mind was guiding me in the direction that I had subconsciously instructed it to go in, which was to avoid writing a book at all costs.

This particular example illustrates that just because you are fearless in one area of your life, it doesn't mean that illogical beliefs aren't holding you back in other areas.

So many people beat themselves up when they procrastinate. They think it is because they don't have the willpower or because they are simply not courageous enough. The answer lies in their beliefs and the fact that they are getting secondary benefits.

Most people never realize that they are actually getting huge secondary benefits from overeating, procrastinating, not expressing their emotions, or not following their dreams. It is a lost cause to try to overcome these secondary gains with pure willpower, and this is why so many people fail to take action towards reaching their goals.

In chapter 6 we will take a deep look at your beliefs, and you will uncover what sort of secondary gains you are getting from doing certain things in your life.

Once you become aware of the beliefs that are really running the show and eliminate the ones that are no longer serving you, it feels like you are no longer going through life with your brakes on.

Some signs that your limiting beliefs are currently controlling you without your being aware of it:

- You know exactly what you need to do on an intellectual level, but for some reason you never go ahead and do it.

- You have the feeling that there is some power inside of you that is controlling you, and no matter how hard you try to reach your goals, this power always ends up choosing what you should do instead.

- You are constantly experiencing the same challenge over and over again.

- It seems like every time you take a step forward, you somehow end up taking two steps back.

- You feel powerless and in doubt when you think about some of the things you want to achieve in life.

I know it seems like you are making conscious decisions, but you are not. You are simply reacting to external situations according to what your specific beliefs dictate. Since you are not aware of most of your beliefs, you are not really directing anything.

I want you to understand that the justifications you are aware of have nothing to do with the way you react. It is the beliefs you are not aware of that are determining both your reaction and your justification.

Please read this one more time and do it slowly, it is crucial that you get this.

- If you are usually negative you can, and will, find something to complain about.

- If you have a pattern of criticizing people, you will do so regardless of the person you are interacting with.

- If you are afraid of getting hurt, you will always bring with you your tough façade that works as armor.

- If you are afraid of being rejected, you will consistently have problems putting yourself on the line.

The external world makes very little difference. Once the initial honeymoon period of a given external environment has passed, you will go right back to your old way of thinking and behaving. You are having the same experience over and over again.

What if I were to call you an idiot for believing your justifications?

Do you really have any control over what happens within you when you read that? Or are your interpretations taking control and choosing the reaction you should have?

By the way, I only wrote that for illustration purposes, and I really think you are a wonderful person (watch your reaction now and see if you chose it consciously).

We have so many automatic reactions and we still wonder why we are suffering. We walk around in our robotic states, and we don't understand why we don't feel the passion, gratitude, and bliss we have always desired.

Your brain is the most powerful piece of machinery here on Earth. It can be your greatest helper or your greatest enemy. Whether it is the former or the latter depends on the meanings you have created and are creating at any given point in time.

Most people are running completely outdated and negative beliefs on a machine that was built to innovate, create, and explore.

How Are Beliefs Created?

If you stand in a pool and look down on your feet from above the water, you will notice that your feet look bigger than usual. There is nothing miraculous about this phenomenon; it is just an optical illusion.

In fact, the ability to see something is the result of a series of events that occur between the eyes, the brain, and the external world. The simplified explanation of how we see is that light is reflected from an object to the cornea of our eye. It then continuous to move through the lens, which focuses it, travels all the way to the retina, and then reaches the brain, where the signal is interpreted. Therefore, it is essential that light travel from the object and to your eyes in order for you to see something. Under water, however, light travels differently than it does through air.

When light passes from water to air, it acts like a magnifying glass, and consequently, everything under water will seem closer than it really is, making your feet look bigger than they really are.

Now imagine standing in a pool and suddenly experiencing short-term memory loss. You would accept the size of the feet that you see in the pool as an accurate depiction of reality. You are accepting an optical illusion as the truth because this is the way you are interpreting it at that moment.

I understand that your illusions and justifications seem to be completely true. I understand that you want to hold on to them and that it is hard to suddenly throw away the foundations of your life.

In order to become truly free, however, you need to give up your current interpretations of the world. You don't need to give them up permanently, you just need to be willing to accept that they are really just subjective interpretations that you have made and that they are not necessarily true. You need to be willing to look inside yourself and be honest.

When you realize that your beliefs have been running most of your life, it can be an overwhelming experience. At this point it is important to continue the awareness process by contemplating where your beliefs come from to begin with.

It gets really interesting when you find out that the majority of your beliefs weren't chosen consciously. In fact, most of them were created through your upbringing, social circle, or society.

Beliefs Always Start with a Single Thought or Interpretation of the World

Maybe you were a little rascal when you were a child and you loved running around and playing with everyone. Perhaps this eventually led to a scolding by your parents and the message that you should sit quietly in your place. Your parents might have acted in this way because they were worried you would be harmed or because they wanted you to be "presentable." As a perfect, free spirit who just wanted to have fun, you didn't view the situation from that perspective.

Most of your beliefs were created by your interpreting rather small and insignificant events and then creating stories around them. If this interpretation wasn't reinforced, nothing more would happen and it would slowly fade away. However, if your interpretation of an event was reinforced, you would slowly find more and more evidence to back it up. Before you knew it, you had a belief with many other beliefs to support it.

Do you really think that all of our negative beliefs magically disappeared just because we grew bigger and started calling ourselves adults?

Your parents, your classmates, what neighborhood your grew up in, what society or period of time you were born in, and so many other factors were not things you chose consciously. Who you "are" is based on meanings that are running in the back of your mind, and at the same time, you had no real say in what created these meanings to begin with. Most of them were created by random external circumstances and events.

Yet here you are, all grown up and still trying to defend and live up to some illusion that has nothing to do with who you are. Some illusion that is so random that it could have been completely different if you had grown up on another street, gone to a different class, or had a different best friend.

All the meanings we learned changed our lives forever; they not only affected the past, they are still affecting us to this day and telling us what we can or can't do in life. They are telling us how we should or shouldn't act and what we have and don't have permission to do.

You absolutely know who you are! You know what you can or can't achieve. You know these things because you believe your interpretations of what the world is like.

How much more intelligent and capable are you right now compared to when you were 5 or 6 years old?

I am willing to bet that you have developed a lot since you were that age. What is fascinating, however, is that most people still carry around with them interpretations of the world that were created when they were just a kid.

This means that decisions and interpretations made by a 5-year-old brain are affecting your life right now. It means that interpretations you made when you were 13 are still running your life. Do you really want the limiting beliefs of a teenager running your life?

Most people never sit down and choose who they want to be. This is what I am urging you to do! It is time to make a conscious decision and choose which interpretations of the world you want to keep and which ones you feel are no longer serving you.

It is time to realize that you are the master of your universe. That your power as the interpreter of external events allows you to create any meanings you like.

It is time to realize that as long as you are living a fairy tale, you might as well be the king or queen who lives happily ever after instead of the peasant who is always suffering. You can either decide to reclaim this inherent power or you can keep the beliefs that are currently causing you pain for another 10 or 15 years and see where that takes you.

The choice is yours . . .

CHAPTER 3
What Are You Focusing On?

One of the recurring themes in this book is that our experience is an internal one, even though most people think it is largely based on the external world.

We have already looked at the obvious reason why our experience is internal: The meanings we create in any given second create a subjective interpretation of external events. Therefore, people can, and will, have completely different experiences of the same external event depending on what attitudes they have.

However, the rabbit hole goes a lot deeper. In order to fully comprehend the impact our internal world is having on the external world, we need to understand how our brain functions.

We are constantly receiving a staggering number of stimuli, and our brains simply can't process all of this information at once. This means that your brain needs to have a filtering system in place so that trying to make sense of too much information at once doesn't overwhelm it. This filtering system is called the reticular activating system (RAS).

The RAS consists of a bundle of closely packed nerve cells that are located in the central core of the brainstem. The RAS functions in a truly ingenious way. It checks through all of the incoming impulses and filters out the ones that it perceive as not being important to you.

This means that you are only experiencing a small percentage of the external world at any given time and you are stripping away all the other impulses in order to focus on what is "important."

The fascinating part about the RAS lies in how it determines what is important to you. It will base the level of importance of a given impulse on the level of alignment it has with your beliefs and values.

This is why you can walk past the same place hundreds of times and miss something that someone else spots the first time. Your beliefs define that given thing as unimportant, while the other person obviously perceives it as having some sort of importance and therefore their brain doesn't filter it out.

Professor Richard Wiseman executed a ten-year study to determine the nature of luck and published his findings in *The Luck Factor: The Scientific Study of the Lucky Mind*. One of the really interesting tests he conducted that highlighted the power of the RAS was the following:

He brought in two groups of people. One of the groups consisted of people who saw themselves as lucky, and the other group consisted of people who thought they were unlucky.

Professor Wiseman asked the participants to count the number of photographs in a sample newspaper. Interestingly, subjects who defined themselves as lucky had a significantly greater chance of noticing a message on page 2 that was disguised as a half-page advertisement in large capital letters: STOP COUNTING— THERE ARE 43 PHOTOGRAPHS IN THIS NEWSPAPER.

Because this group perceived themselves as lucky, their RAS looked for evidence of this, and consequently they had a much greater chance of finding this message.

In essence, you are filtering out the majority of things that are not in accordance with your beliefs and keeping the things that reinforce your existing beliefs.

Guess what this means?

If you think that you have a hard time connecting with people, your mind is constantly going to feed you evidence of this. You could even have a really deep connection with someone, and still your mind is going to give you evidence that you don't.

You might tell yourself that the person just wanted to get something from you, that they were just being polite, that they were faking it. People will find the most incredible justifications in order to reinforce their beliefs about a situation.

Likewise, if you think people are out to scam you, your mind is constantly going to focus on finding evidence that reinforces this. This means that even if someone is very honest and truly looking for a win-win situation, you are going to find some sort of "proof" that they might be trying to scam you.

You might tell yourself that there was something fishy about that person or that his offer seemed too good to be true.

You could also be cocky and have the belief that no one can ever scam you, which would lead to your turning a blind eye to the people who are consistently stealing from you.

If you wear a new dress or suit that you believe makes you look attractive, you are going to find a lot of evidence for it when you go out. You will feel like members of the opposite sex are checking you out, flirting with you, or that people are a lot nicer. Isn't it weird how this feeling suddenly goes away after you have worn that dress or suit a couple of times?

Either your clothing is of low quality and gets worn out very quickly, or you are no longer scanning for the same kind of evidence because you don't feel your clothes have that "shiny new" feeling anymore.

Transformation Exercise

Go online and search for "selective attention test" by Professor Daniel Simons and Christopher Chabris. This is a world-famous awareness test in video form and is about 1 to 2 minutes long. If you can, please watch this video before reading any further.

When watching the selective-attention test video, most people will see the obvious details. However, when people focus fully on counting the passes, the gorilla is missed in about 50% of cases. This is the RAS in action!

The stronger a given belief becomes, the more evidence you are going to find to reinforce it, which again makes the belief even stronger.

It is a self-fulfilling prophecy. If you have had the belief that you don't deserve to be with beautiful women for the past 20 years, that belief has had a lot of time to be reinforced, and I can almost guarantee that it has been very hard for you to meet attractive women.

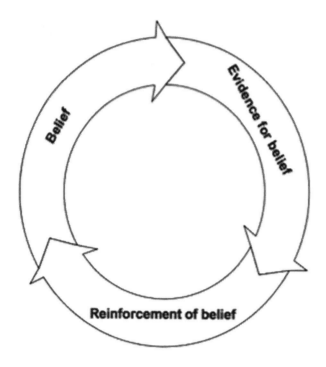

The Principle of Reinforcement

The principle of reinforcement works in two ways. For illustration purposes, we are going to use the belief that someone thinks he doesn't deserve to be with beautiful women,

Principle 1

He has become so accustomed to this belief that subconsciously he will seek out situations that reinforce it.

Principle 2

He believes that he doesn't deserve to be with beautiful women on such a deep level that he subconsciously compels any attractive woman he meets to reject him, even though she actually likes him to begin with. This second principle functions through your subcommunication and micropatterns of behavior that most people can't perceive consciously but pick up on intuitively.

An example of these two principles is when this man, who has the belief that "I don't deserve to be with beautiful women," approaches a really attractive woman.

Now he might not even be aware that he has this belief, and maybe he has justified it by telling himself that attractive women are all bitches. In spite of this, he gets himself really pumped up and approaches her with a "clever" pickup line.

The moment she looks at him and starts processing what he said, he will become nervous and start fidgeting, twitching an eye, turning the body away (getting ready to be rejected), or some other small thing. This is principle 2 in action.

Now the woman might even like him, but she will pick up on what happens either intuitively or consciously and in most cases, she will reject him. If you ask her about it afterwards, she will probably say that something just wasn't right about that guy.

Because this guy's limiting belief is so deeply rooted, he will subconsciously "make" her reject him (principle 2).

Let's say she really likes him a lot and decides to give him a chance, even though there is something off about him. It is almost guaranteed that he is subconsciously going to set up blocks for himself during the interaction because it goes against his existing belief system.

These blocks can be extreme nervousness, unexplainable fear, blanking out completely, or saying strange things he wouldn't usually say. This is just his mind's way of telling this man that he has no business being with an attractive woman and that he should get out of there as quickly as possible.

For the sake of this example, let's pretend that this woman still likes him and gives him her number. Chances are that he won't call her because he will find all sorts of "evidence" to support his belief that "I don't deserve to be with beautiful women."

Examples:

- She only talked with me and gave me her number to be nice.

- It is probably a fake number, so I am not even going to try calling.

- If I call her I won't know what to say.

- I don't even know where to take her if she does answer and says yes.

- I am just going to make a fool of myself. She is not going to remember me.

This is all principle 1 at work, by the way; he is trying to keep himself out of a situation that could go against his belief that he does not deserve attractive women. He achieves this by never calling her and thereby not letting her "accept" him, something that would go against his beliefs.

For the sake of this example, I want you to imagine that he somehow overcame his excuses and called her despite his underlying belief that he doesn't deserve to be with a woman who is attractive. They subsequently go on a date. Let's even say that during the date they somehow end up really liking each other and decide that they should have a relationship.

The relationship might be really good in the beginning. However, if this man continues to believe that he doesn't deserve

Mateo Tabatabai

to be with a beautiful woman, there is going to be a misalignment between his belief and the external world.

Therefore, his mind will start looking for proof for why he needs to get out of the relationship so that he can be aligned with his belief again. He might become really controlling, jealous, or overly needy. He might stop taking care of himself and become really lazy, or he might start making up reasons why she is not good enough for him.

Either way, he is subconsciously going to sabotage the relationship and break up with her or push her so far away that she leaves him. When this happens, there is an alignment between his belief and the external world once again and he can relax.

Before he gets all the way back into his comfort zone, however, he is going to justify the idea that all beautiful women are really bitches and that he was right all along. This justification keeps him from digging any further and finding the underlying limiting belief.

But why would he go through all this trouble to reinforce his limiting belief? Because he is getting a secondary benefit from the belief of being undeserving, and therefore the mind thinks that this belief is protecting him. We don't know what secondary benefit(s) this particular guy is getting from his limiting belief, but some examples could be:

- An attractive woman will cheat on me and hurt me.

- Attractive women have a lot of options, and I don't want to compete with other men all the time.

- I am not sexually confident enough to please an attractive woman.

51

- Attractive women are all really confident, and I don't feel like I am in control if I am in a relationship with an independent woman.

If he can avoid all these scenarios which he has created in his mind by having the belief that he doesn't deserve to be with an attractive woman, is it really that surprising that he is going to reinforce his "protective" limiting belief?

Have you ever had an experience like this? Have you ever started earning more money than you were comfortable with and then somehow sabotaged it?

Have you ever become more fit and healthy than you thought was "right" and then unexplainably started eating a lot of junk food and quitting all the habits that got you there?

Do you have a pattern of somehow messing up relationships the moment they start going really well and you truly start connecting with someone? The reason why you do this is because your mind thinks you are getting a much larger secondary benefit by avoiding certain actions that you logically view as being positive.

I hope you are starting to see the seriousness of the beliefs you have and how your brain will do anything to reinforce them by constantly finding evidence to support them. If you don't change your beliefs, it doesn't matter how much willpower you have, it is going to feel like you are trying to climb a very slippery slope. Every time you start getting the feel of it, you are going to slide down and end up where you started.

If you have the belief that it is hard to find a spouse you can trust, your mind is going to find evidence for exactly that and filter out all the things that are not in alignment with your belief.

If you think being healthy is a full-time job, that is exactly what you are going to get. If you think making money is hard, that people are evil, that life is a struggle, or that you can't be happy all the time, this is exactly what your mind is going to find evidence for and reinforce.

Beliefs ---» What you focus on and find evidence for ---» Reinforcement of beliefs

I have seen so many women who talk about how they can never find a good man who won't lie, cheat, or be abusive. Surprisingly, they somehow keep ending up with men who do just that!

I have seen so many people complain about how unlucky they are and how something bad always happens to them. Is it really so surprising when what they have secretly been "wishing" for finally shows up?

Then there are the people who view the world as an unjust place. For some reason they are always in some sort of struggle against the injustice of the world, and it always ends up with their being treated in an unfair way.

Transformation Exercise

Take the time to answer the following question:

What are some of my limiting beliefs that seem to be continuously reinforced?

I want you to really get that your current results mean nothing with regard to who you are or who you can be. Your current results in life are merely an indication of what sort of beliefs you have entertained up to this point.

It is not because you are struggling financially that you are bad with money. It is because you have the belief that you are bad with money that you are struggling financially.

It is not because you don't have a loving spouse that you are not worthy of love. It is because you believe that you are not worthy of love that you don't have a loving spouse.

It is not because you are constantly walking into things that you are clumsy. It is because you have the belief that you are clumsy that you are constantly walking into things.

When you understand that your beliefs are responsible for your external results, you can use this knowledge as a tool for introspection. Most people will have a hard time just identifying all of their limiting beliefs because they are simply not aware of them, and this is why I originally came up with this exercise.

Because your beliefs are responsible for external results, the lack of results in a given area of life is a very good indication that you have limiting beliefs in that area. Therefore, I want you to make a list of the areas of your life that are important to you but simply aren't meeting your expectations. Doing this will create some awareness and help you find some of the limiting beliefs that are holding you back.

Transformation Exercise

Write down all the areas in which you have wanted or tried to succeed but always seemed to come up short.

Because these areas are typically also going to be the areas in which you have limiting beliefs, I want you to try to find some of those limiting beliefs.

You really need to understand that your beliefs are what have been causing you to come up short. It is not because you don't have the talent or willpower or worth to succeed in the areas that are important to you; it is just that you have had beliefs that are not very constructive to achieving a certain goal.

Therefore, you need to start shifting the thoughts/meanings/ beliefs you are entertaining at any given point to more positive internal structures.

When you start playing around with the world of meaning instead of letting it play you, you are going to transform your entire life. Change the internal structure and you will automatically redesign the external one.

> **"When patterns are broken,**
> **new worlds emerge."**
> **—Tuli Kupferberg**

Playing with Meaning

If you take the meaning out of something, you are also going to take the emotion out of it because it no longer means anything. The meanings you create are deeply connected with the emotions you feel. Therefore, it is essential that you take control of your "meaning-making skills" if you ever want to take control of your emotions.

The meanings you create in your mind are going to create the emotions you feel, and the emotions you feel on a day-to-day basis are going to determine the quality of your life. Hence, you can immediately change the quality of your life by changing the meanings you create, which in turn changes the emotions you feel.

Realizing what sort of meanings you are currently creating in your life is very simple. All you have to do is ask yourself what you are consistently focusing on and what type of internal representations you are making.

Here are some examples of the correlation between meaning and emotion:

- When fans go completely crazy watching a grudge match between the two top rivals in a given league. Because there is a much deeper meaning to this specific match compared to a regular match against other teams, a lot more emotion is going to be involved.

- When you celebrate your anniversary with your spouse. In reality, this is just like any other day of the year. However, because of the meaning you associate with this day, a lot of emotion is going to be involved.

Think of something that you absolutely love to do and are really passionate about. I want you to find one of those niche hobbies that you really enjoy doing and ask yourself, "How does performing this activity make me feel?"

What if you were to try to explain how great that hobby is to someone who is not interested in it?

Chances are they wouldn't have anything near the emotional response you have. This is simply because they don't attach the same meaning to that activity that you do.

The connection between meaning and emotion is pretty obvious. In fact, it is so simple that people are usually not consciously aware of it. Most people don't understand that their meanings are creating the emotions they feel. Instead, they assume that external events and experiences are creating the emotions.

The meanings you create are changing your internal world by giving you certain emotions, and they are changing the external world by deciding what you focus on (the RAS).

As human beings, we like to create associations between things. If you experience happiness nine out of ten times on your birthday, you are automatically going to assume it is your birthday that is giving you happiness.

If you feel empowered when you go to the gym, you are going to assume that it is the activity of going to the gym that gives you a feeling of empowerment. If you feel a deep sense of connection whenever someone tells you that they love you, you are going to assume that it is the declaration of love that gives you the sense of connection.

If it was in fact the external event that created the emotion, then how come we have people who hate their birthdays? Are there people who go to the gym and feel completely lazy instead of empowered (I know, I have been here a couple of times)? How come some people will cringe and withdraw emotionally when you declare your love for them?

Whether you feel happy or unhappy on your birthday depends completely on the meaning you attach to the external event of a birthday.

Whether you feel empowered or lazy in the gym will depend solely on the type of internal representations you are making about the activity of working out.

A declaration of love can either mean connection or becoming too vulnerable, depending on the interpretations you make.

Another example of the correlation between meaning and emotion is when people have irrational fears. Someone who is afraid to fly simply has a different interpretation of flying than the person who doesn't mind flying.

Every second of your life you are creating meanings and interpretations for what a given external event means to you.

Because meaning and emotion are deeply connected, your emotions are typically going to be in complete alignment with the meaning you have created. If you create the meaning that you have been treated unfairly, it is very likely that you are going to experience emotions that are at the negative end of the spectrum.

Likewise, if you create the meaning that someone really loves and cares for you, you are going to experience positive emotions that are in alignment with that interpretation of the world. I understand that for some people it can be hard to fully accept that this is really how the world functions.

After all, what if you lose your job, someone laughs at you, someone insults you, or whatever you perceive to be a tragedy occurs in your life? Surely any one of these would be a perfect example of an external event that is going to affect your internal experience negatively?

Well, it only affects you negatively because you choose to create an internal story about the event that creates negative emotions instead of positive ones.

Meaning that could result in a negative emotion:

When someone insults me, they are trying to dominate me mentally and make me feel inferior to them.

Meaning that could result in a positive emotion:

When someone insults me, they are begging me to give them the attention and compassion they lack in their lives.

Meaning that could result in a negative emotion:

If I lose my job, it means I am a reject who is not capable of anything.

Meaning that could result in a positive emotion:

If I lose my job, it is because my boss thought I wasn't living up to my full potential working in that position and that I have a bigger purpose in life. In fact, he was trying to push me to grow and develop.

Meaning that could result in a negative emotion:

When someone laughs while looking at me, they are mocking me, and it means that I am not living up to a certain standard.

Meaning that could result in a positive emotion:

When someone laughs while looking at me, it is because I am a beam of light and I bring joy and laughter to the life of him/her.

I am going to repeat this point: The emotions that are affecting the quality of your life are not really coming from the external world. The events themselves are not responsible for the emotions we feel. There are only neutral events in external reality, and you give them a negative or positive meaning.

As a result, you decide which emotion you should feel, exactly as in the example of dog meat being a delicacy in some countries and the cause of disgust and sadness in others. ALL of your emotions and thoughts are coming from you.

If the negative emotion you feel isn't from you, then how come you are carrying it around with you and it seems to follow you everywhere you go? If your anger is really caused by another person, then how come it can stay with you even when this person is no longer present?

YOU are carrying the emotion around with you. YOU are the cause of the emotion and most importantly, YOU have the power to stop or start feeling any emotion at ANY time, regardless of your external circumstances.

Transformation Exercise

Deep-Rooted Anger

Make sure you are in a place where you are comfortable. I want you to stand up and remember a time in your life when you were really angry. I want you to really allow this anger to come up.

Don't judge it or analyze it, just acknowledge that it is there and allow yourself to become as angry as you possibly can. Remember all the details of this specific event and really get into the state of anger. Think of what happened that made you so angry, stand, and breathe exactly as you would if you were really angry. Focus on the thoughts you would focus on when you are in this angry state.

Feel the anger as deeply as you possibly can for a few minutes, until you feel you no longer want to stay with that emotion. Make sure to physically shake it off when you are done and just let it go. Please do this exercise now, before you move on.

Deep-Rooted Gratitude

Now I want you to do something a little different. Stand up and remember a time in your life that really gave you a feeling of gratitude. I want you to remember this gratitude in as many details as you possibly can.

I want you to stand and breathe in the way you would when you are in this state of gratitude. Focus on the thoughts you would focus on when you are in this state. Feel the appreciation in every part of your body and stay with it for as long as you like.

Go ahead and do this exercise now.

You decide what emotions you feel by deciding what interpretations you are making and what you are focusing on in any given second of your life. It doesn't matter on what end of the emotional spectrum you currently feel you are, there is always room to feel either better or worse, and it all depends on the interpretations you make.

It is crucial that you start taking responsibility for your thoughts and emotions. Claiming this responsibility is the only way you can reclaim your personal power and be able to make conscious choices and decisions instead of just reacting to whatever comes up.

So many people are searching for their talents and God-given gifts; meanwhile they are missing the biggest and most obvious one. They are missing the fact that they are the creator of their own destiny, in the sense that they are literally designing their experience of life through the meanings they create.

I know of no feat as powerful as being able to consciously shape your experience just by changing your perspective and playing with the world of meaning.

Typical objections the mind will make

On the subject of taking complete responsibility for the thoughts and emotions you have, there are some common questions and objections.

1. This is completely unrealistic; you can't just create any meaning you want with no regard to what is actually going on in the external world.

This objection always puts a smile on my face. What do you think you are already doing?

Let's look at some of the interpretations people are typically making:

- I am not good enough.

- I am not very attractive.

- I am such a clumsy person.

- Nobody ever takes me seriously.

- I just don't have enough confidence to do that.

- I am not talented enough.

- I don't deserve to be loved.

- I am never going to amount to anything.

- I am really lazy.

- I am not disciplined enough.

- I have a temper and I often have uncontrollable anger fits.

- I am always sick.

- It is such a cruel world out there.

- There are no people that I can relate to in this place.

- Most people just don't understand me.

What is the difference between what you are already doing and what I am asking you to do? Do you really think that half of the things you are telling yourself on a daily basis are true?

Are you really telling me that when your meanings give you unhappiness they are realistic and when they are created in a way where they can only give you happiness they are unrealistic?

Since there is no objective truth, the real question is whether you are going to create meanings that are improving the quality of your life or decreasing it.

I am not asking you to use the power of meaning to become an arrogant or cocky person who never listens to others or isn't open to feedback.

I am simply encouraging you to take two steps: Stop using the meanings you create to demoralize yourself, and start using the meanings you create to empower yourself!

2. Are you asking me to only feel happy emotions and walk around like I am enlightened?

Well, if that is what you want to do, by all means go for it. It sure doesn't sound too bad to me. All joking aside, there is one thing that I want to make completely clear. Choosing the meanings you create is not about suppressing your anger, sadness, or grief. In fact, when I say negative emotions, I am only referring to emotions that are decreasing the quality of your life.

It is my belief that no emotion is bad and that all emotions have their purpose. Just because an emotion like sadness is not constructive in one situation, that doesn't mean it isn't extremely relevant at other times. In fact, an emotion like sadness or anger can be very effective when it comes to giving your system a flush and cleaning everything out.

Suppressing your emotions can haunt you later in life in the form of disease, and it is definitely not something I will recommend you do. The problem is not the emotion; the problem is the context in which you use the emotion.

Most people suppress a given emotion when it is actually appropriate, and then they carry it around with them for weeks, months, or even years. If you really want to feel emotions of sadness, anger, and even depression, then go for it! Let it flush your system and then let it go.

The reason why these emotions are causing people so much suffering is because they are not content with just feeling the emotion. They also have to create a negative story around it, start identifying with it, and carry it around with them as if it was an emblem of achievement. People tend to make emotions a part of their identity, instead of just seeing them as energy that is passing through their body.

If someone you love passes away, let sadness do its job. It is only natural to feel grief for the personal loss you have suffered. When you have felt all the sadness you need to feel, it is time to create a more positive interpretation of what happened.

For example:

- How would this person want me to deal with this if he/she was still here?

- What can I learn from this event that can make me appreciate the people who are still with me even more?

- What are some things I absolutely need to do before I pass away?

Most people take another route, and that is to completely or partially suppress their emotions and then build a story about how unfair it is and how they just can't allow themselves to feel any positive emotions without this person.

They then carry this story around with them everywhere they go. It is almost as if it was not enough that someone they loved passed away; now they also have to continuously punish themselves for it. By doing this, they decrease the quality of not only their own life, but also the lives of their loved ones.

3. Life isn't only good, so why should I create good meanings about things?

Well, it doesn't really matter to me if you do or you don't. I am simply pointing out to you that you have the ability to live an even more incredible life than you are already doing. Whether you use that ability or not is completely up to you.

4. How do I start doing this in my life?

This is the kind of question I really love to hear. Are you ready to start using your powers to create a truly magical experience? Then let's move on.

Because most people don't understand the power they possess in each moment of their life, they don't feel like they have any real control over the quality of their life. True power lies in being able to constantly change the meanings you create to the ones that serve you best and flow with any external event instead of trying to resist it.

The first step to becoming a master of meaning is to fully recognize that none of your beliefs and meanings are absolutely true. Sure, I might have meanings that I believe in very strongly (like the theories I am sharing with you in this book), but I also accept the fact that my human brain is fallible and that I can very well be completely wrong in many of the things I believe.

Are you willing to try on the "no truth" frame of mind for a couple of days? If you don't like it, you can always come back and pick up your old truths again.

When you have this frame of mind, you no longer have any reason to try to convince others that your beliefs are true. You no longer have a need to argue with people in order to prove that you are right.

How much is it going to improve your life quality to know that, in a sense, everyone is right and there is no point in arguing or trying to defend your specific truth? Even racists who say you can define someone's value by the color of their skin are right, in the sense that they actually believe the beliefs they have adopted.

When we get in arguments over who is right, our ego takes over and it usually gives us nothing but suffering. The funny thing is, most people don't even understand that they are not really arguing with a person when they get caught in a heated discussion.

What's really going on is that their beliefs are arguing with the beliefs of the person in front of them. Does it really matter what random belief is right?

You have people arguing about whether the lion is really the king of the jungle, and while they are stressing and fussing, the lion is lying somewhere in the savannah enjoying life. The lion doesn't care whether it is the king, so why do you?

Only by understanding that it is all just meanings and representations will you be free to create new and more empowering interpretations.

> **"Seeing is not believing;**
> **believing is seeing. You see things**
> **not as they are, but as you are."**
> **—Eric Butterworth**

The Rules of the Game

It is time to start playing with your meanings and interpretations. We are going to do this by examining the rules you have set up for yourself. All human beings have rules they play by.

When you are not aware of your meaning-making skills, you are typically not going to notice these rules and how they are affecting your life.

These rules are basically just beliefs; I just refer to them as rules because they determine when you are "winning" and when you are "losing" in life.

You have rules for when you are loved, when you are financially independent, when you are a good parent, when you are a good spouse, when you are ethical, when you are a good lover, when you look like a fool, and so on.

You have rules for every single area of your life, and every time you enter a new arena you are going to set up some new ground rules as quickly as possible. These rules are not universal by any means. In fact, quite the opposite is true, and each person has their own unique set of rules about things.

Let's look at some examples of rules someone could have:

Rules for when someone loves me—When someone loves me they are always honest with me, they are nice to me, they protect me, they open the door for me, they remember my birthday, they don't yell at me, they always say how much they love me . . .

Rules for when I look like a fool—If people look at me weird, if I stumble on a rock, if I stutter, if I don't know what to say, if I don't dance like a pro, if I am put on the spot and I blush . . .

Rules for when I am a good lover—If the other person moans really loudly, if they climax three or more times, if they tell me that I am the best lover they have had without my asking them, if they constantly want to have sex with me . . .

Rules for when I am unethical—If I say no to someone and they genuinely need my help, if I say something that makes someone else sad, if I find a wallet and keep the money . . . .

Rules for when I am financially independent—When I own a lot of big houses around the world, when I no longer have to work, when I have enough money to do whatever I want, when I can travel the world . . .

Rules for when I am happy—When all my other rules are upheld, when I am really fit, when I am really healthy, and when everyone loves me or at least likes me.

Your rules are, in reality, just beliefs about when you have "made it" in a given area of your life. This means that if you are not fulfilling your unique rules for when you are happy, you are subconsciously not going to allow yourself to feel a high level of happiness.

The problem with this approach is that all of your rules are completely subjective and based on interpretations you just happened to make by chance.

Most people have their rules set up in a way that makes it almost impossible for them to succeed. A typical example of this is if someone's rule for happiness is "I feel happy when I am successful, wealthy, and healthy and my relationships are all working perfectly."

The problem is, most people don't know their rules for success, wealth, health, or relationships. So what they are actually saying is "I will be happy when all these things that I can never measure are fulfilled." You can probably see it is going to be problematic if you can never feel a high level of happiness because you have completely abstract rules for when you can allow yourself to feel this emotion.

Most people are completely unaware of the rules they have in the different areas of their life. Even the people who are somewhat aware of their rules usually make two mistakes:

1. They choose criteria that aren't measurable. Let's say one of your criteria for being rich is "When I have enough money so that I can live my ideal lifestyle without having to work."

With a criterion like that, you are setting yourself up for failure because your idea of the ideal lifestyle is going to change over time and with it, the amount of money you will need will change.

2. The second mistake people make is that their criteria are so far from where they currently are, it is going to take a lot of hard work and time to get to the point of fulfilling them.

Sure, it's great to have big goals, but if your happiness or sense of wealth is dependent on a really big goal, you are cheating yourself out of feeling those emotions during the journey towards reaching your goal.

Let's take an example with the rules for when someone loves you. "When someone loves me they are always honest with me, they are nice to me, they protect me, they open the door for me, they remember my birthday, they don't yell at me, they always say how much they love me . . ." What do any of these rules really mean?

Imagine that I had a shop that sold the perfect spouse who would always love you. All you had to do was pay a one-time fee and give me your list of rules for when someone loves you. I would then go ahead and mold your perfect partner, who would always make you feel loved and wanted.

With the rules you have for love, this means that I would fulfill your order if I delivered a spouse with the following criteria:

- This partner has a built-in lie detector so you can see if he is honest or not.

- He never expresses his true opinions just to be nice to you.

- He is an ultimate fighter/army specialist who can protect you against anything from hurricanes to ninjas.

- He works part-time as a doorman and therefore is an expert in opening the door for you.

- He has a built-in calendar system and will automatically sing happy birthday to you on your birthday.

- He always speaks in a monotone in order to not sound like he is yelling, and last but not least, he says he loves you even when he doesn't mean it!

I know I am being a little silly and exaggerating things, but I want to show you that the rules most people set can never be fulfilled. They are completely abstract and there is no logic behind them. They are something you were programmed to believe and you never bothered to change.

Even on the rare occasion that they are all achieved, you are still going to find something you aren't happy with. Can you just imagine the scenario where your spouse fulfilled all of your rules? You would probably grow tired of him and complain to your friends about how there is no spontaneity or adventure in your relationship anymore.

When this happens, you are in fact just setting up new rules because your old rules have now been fulfilled!

I think we have all tried doing this on some level, and a good example of this is in the area of money. If you look at your financial goals and how much you need to be making in order to feel wealthy, you will see that it is constantly changing. If you start with the goal of wanting to earn $100,000 a year, you are typically going to change it to something much higher once you actually reach this goal.

You will of course justify this as a miscalculation, that $100,000 a year really isn't enough to be wealthy in this day and age.

Now the fascinating aspect is that you are using these completely arbitrary beliefs to determine whether you have "permission" to feel happy, successful, and loved. The real question to ask is "Why have I made my rules so hard to fulfill when I can just change them to some other subjective criteria?"

When you realize there is no absolute truth in the criteria you currently have, you are free to change the criteria so it becomes easier to fulfill your rules and consequently feel a given positive emotion.

I can virtually guarantee you that everyone I meet likes me and wants me to grow as a person. Is it because my hypnosis skills allow me to program their mind, or is it that I am just so charming?

The answer is none of the above. I know that everyone I meet will like me and want me to grow because my rules for these two concepts are very simple.

Mateo's Rules

How I know if someone likes me—If they look at me, say anything to me, or were born on planet Earth.

71

How I know if someone wants me to grow as a person— If they try to give me negative emotions so I can overcome a challenge, if they try to give me positive emotions to show me I am on the right track, and, of course, if they were born on planet Earth.

Most people will call both of these rules delusional, and they are absolutely right. My rules for when someone likes me and when someone wants me to grow are completely delusional and out of touch with reality. But so are everyone else's rules; this is why it is called **SUBJECTIVE** reality.

It is all just interpretations anyway, and if you ask me, I would much rather play the game of life feeling as many positive states as possible because everyone likes me and everyone wants me to grow.

Can I prove that my rules are real? Absolutely not. Do they serve me and make me feel good compared to having more "realistic" rules? Absolutely. Do I constantly find evidence for them because of the power of focus and reinforcement? Absolutely. Do people automatically react to me differently when I have these beliefs? Absolutely. Do I love these two rules? You bet I love them!

Setting up your rules in this way isn't about growing complacent and never achieving anything. It is about feeling good while you go for the things you want in life.

Why delay your positive emotions just because some mind-made criteria have to be fulfilled? Just change the criteria and feel whatever it is you want to feel right now!

This is not about cheating yourself and pretending something is good when it is not. This is about completely changing the rules of the game.

When you change the rules of the game, you are going to focus on different things and therefore feel different emotions. These are genuine emotions and not something you are tricking yourself into feeling.

Examples:

Old rule for gratitude: I am grateful when everything in my life is good, when I am successful, when I am healthy, when I am growing every day, and when I feel a connection to God.

New rule for gratitude: I am grateful when I have life pumping through my veins.

Are we cheating ourselves into feeling grateful here? Of course not. We are simply changing our focus. In the old rule, we miss the bigger picture and the fact that just being here on planet Earth is a miracle. In the new rule, we don't let a miracle like life be ignored. Why? Because it will allow us to feel a genuine and deep gratitude for being alive.

> **"People usually consider walking on water or in thin air a miracle. But I think the real miracle is not to walk either on water or in thin air, but to walk on earth. Every day we are engaged in a miracle which we don't even recognize: a blue sky, white clouds, green leaves, the black, curious eyes of a child—our own two eyes. All is a miracle."**
> **—Thich Nhat Hanh**

When people start looking at their rules in life, they often find out they are pursuing things that are not even important to them. So many people are putting off travels, enjoyment and pleasure because they want to become "wealthy."

When they finally change the rules to what they feel is appropriate, they find out they are already wealthy according to the things they want to do in life. They find out they can continue living the lifestyle they want to live without ever having to work again.

If these people hadn't examined their rules, they could have wasted 10 to 20 extra years doing work they didn't necessarily enjoy when they didn't even need the money. I don't know about you, but to me it seems like a very good deal to spend 10 minutes examining your rules and then saving 10 to 20 years!

I will give you an example from one of my own rules and how changing it made me wealthy within just a few minutes.

My previous rule for being wealthy:

- When I have $10 million in my bank account.

- When I own at least 15 houses that are earning me rent money every month.

- When I can buy anything I want without having to think about money.

- When I don't have to work and still have a six-figure income.

Talk about setting myself up for failure and postponing the feeling of wealth! Am I still going to achieve those goals?

Of course I am, and I am going to do so just because making money is nothing but a fun game to me. Do I want to wait until I have achieved all of those things before I can feel wealthy? Of course not!

My new rules for wealth:

- I am wealthy when I can maintain the life quality I currently have for 12 months without having to work.

- I am wealthy when I have the time to travel, exercise, study, and meditate without being limited by a steady job.

- I am wealthy when I am healthy enough to exercise four times a week and do the things I love (martial arts, yoga, dancing) without any physical restrictions.

- I am wealthy when I have at least two ideas I can work on in the areas of life I am passionate about.

- I am wealthy when I express my love to my family and friends whenever I speak to them.

When I first did this I suddenly realized that I was in fact already wealthy. I also had the realization that even if I suddenly won the lottery, my life really wouldn't change that drastically!

When I changed my rules in the area of wealth, it also became a lot easier for me to acquire additional wealth. Since I was already wealthy, I was behaving and feeling like someone who is wealthy.

Do you think it is easier to acquire wealth when you already know you are wealthy?

Most importantly, I gave myself the gratitude I deserved right NOW instead of delaying the positive emotions I could feel because I didn't live up to some imaginary rule I had created in my mind.

All of my rules are constructed so that I am in control of whether or not they are fulfilled. For example, one of my criteria for wealth is "I am wealthy when I express my love to my family and friends." I am in control of whether or not I do this, and it is important that you set your criteria so that you are in control.

If my criterion was "I am wealthy when my family and friends love me," I would be setting myself up for failure because now the control is no longer in my hands.

What if my friend was angry and yelled at me one day and my rule for love stated that someone who yells at you doesn't love you? I would mistakenly come to think that he didn't love me. At this point I will not only feel my friend doesn't love me, but I will no longer feel wealthy either.

This is the power of rules, and it is important that you set them up so that you are in control. I once heard a rule for success which I immediately adopted. This rule is "Every day alive and breathing is success." Talk about setting yourself up for **SUCCESS!**

What if something in the external world happens and my rules for wealth are no longer fulfilled? Well, I just go ahead and change the criteria I have for that given rule. I am an expert meaning maker, and I play in the world of meaning in whatever way will give me the most positive emotions and the highest quality of life.

Exploration of Your Rules

It is time to take a look at the rules you have set up for your life and see whether they are serving you or not. In order to get the most benefit from this exercise, you should take the time to get all of your criteria for each given area of your life down on paper, and yes, I recommend that you actually write down your rules.

You don't have anything to lose, and if you do it right, you can have some major realizations with very little work. Remember that everyone has different rules, and therefore it is important to write down what your specific rules are and not what you think is the "right" answer.

Wealth

What has to be fulfilled before you feel wealthy?

Are your rules in this area of life improving or decreasing the quality of your life?

Do you want to keep the rules in this area of your life or change them?

If you want to change them, go ahead and decide your new rules for this area right now.

Attractiveness

What has to be fulfilled before you feel sexy?

Are your rules in this area of life improving or decreasing the quality of your life?

Do you want to keep the rules in this area of your life or change them?

If you want to change them, go ahead and decide your new rules for this area right now.

Success

What has to be fulfilled before you feel that you are successful in life?

Are your rules in this area of life improving or decreasing the quality of your life?

Do you want to keep the rules in this area of your life or change them?

If you want to change them, go ahead and decide your new rules for this area right now.

Love

What has to be fulfilled before you feel loved?

What has to be fulfilled before you feel you love someone?

Are your rules in this area of life improving or decreasing the quality of your life?

Do you want to keep the rules in this area of your life or change them?

If you want to change them, go ahead and decide your new rules for this area right now.

Trust

What has to be fulfilled before you trust someone else?

Are your rules in this area of life improving or decreasing the quality of your life?

Do you want to keep the rules in this area of your life or change them?

If you want to change them, go ahead and decide your new rules for this area right now.

Anger

What has to be fulfilled before you feel angry?

Are your rules in this area of life improving or decreasing the quality of your life?

Do you want to keep the rules in this area of your life or change them?

If you want to change them, go ahead and decide your new rules for this area right now.

Sadness

What has to be fulfilled before you feel sadness?

Are your rules in this area of life improving or decreasing the quality of your life?

Do you want to keep the rules in this area of your life or change them?

If you want to change them, go ahead and decide your new rules for this area right now.

Abundance

What has to be fulfilled before you feel abundance in life?

Are your rules in this area of life improving or decreasing the quality of your life?

Do you want to keep the rules in this area of your life or change them?

If you want to change them, go ahead and decide your new rules for this area right now.

Scarcity

What has to be fulfilled before you feel scarcity or a lack of something in life?

Are your rules in this area of life improving or decreasing the quality of your life?

Do you want to keep the rules in this area of your life or change them?

If you want to change them, go ahead and decide your new rules for this area right now.

Gratitude

What has to be fulfilled before you feel gratitude in life?

Are your rules in this area of life improving or decreasing the quality of your life?

Do you want to keep the rules in this area of your life or change them?

If you want to change them, go ahead and decide your new rules for this area right now.

Negativity

What has to be fulfilled before you feel negative?

Are your rules in this area of life improving or decreasing the quality of your life?

Do you want to keep the rules in this area of your life or change them?

If you want to change them, go ahead and decide your new rules for this area right now.

Positivity/Optimism

What has to be fulfilled before you feel optimistic?

Are your rules in this area of life improving or decreasing the quality of your life?

Do you want to keep the rules in this area of your life or change them?

If you want to change them, go ahead and decide your new rules for this area right now.

Failure

What has to be fulfilled before you feel you have failed?

Are your rules in this area of life improving or decreasing the quality of your life?

Do you want to keep the rules in this area of your life or change them?

If you want to change them, go ahead and decide your new rules for this area right now.

Sex

What has to be fulfilled before you feel like a great lover?

Are your rules in this area of life improving or decreasing the quality of your life?

Do you want to keep the rules in this area of your life or change them?

If you want to change them, go ahead and decide your new rules for this area right now.

Happiness

What has to be fulfilled before you feel happiness?

Are your rules in this area of life improving or decreasing the quality of your life?

Do you want to keep the rules in this area of your life or change them?

If you want to change them, go ahead and decide your new rules for this area right now.

Friendship

What has to be fulfilled before someone is a true friend to you?

What has to be fulfilled before you feel you are a good friend?

Are your rules in this area of life improving or decreasing the quality of your life?

Do you want to keep the rules in this area of your life or change them?

If you want to change them, go ahead and decide your new rules for this area right now.

Growth

What has to be fulfilled before you feel you are growing and developing?

Are your rules in this area of life improving or decreasing the quality of your life?

Do you want to keep the rules in this area of your life or change them.

If you want to change them, go ahead and decide your new rules for this area right now.

Inner Peace

What has to be fulfilled before you feel peaceful?

Are your rules in this area of life improving or decreasing the quality of your life?

Do you want to keep the rules in this area of your life or change them?

If you want to change them, go ahead and decide your new rules for this area right now.

Career

What has to be fulfilled before you enjoy your career?

Are your rules in this area of life improving or decreasing the quality of your life?

Do you want to keep the rules in this area of your life or change them?

If you want to change them, go ahead and decide your new rules for this area right now.

Health

What has to be fulfilled before you feel healthy?

Are your rules in this area of life improving or decreasing the quality of your life?

Do you want to keep the rules in this area of your life or change them?

If you want to change them, go ahead and decide your new rules for this area right now.

Contribution

What has to be fulfilled before you feel you are contributing to the world or to others?

Are your rules in this area of life improving or decreasing the quality of your life?

Do you want to keep the rules in this area of your life or change them?

If you want to change them, go ahead and decide your new rules for this area right now.

Relationships

What has to be fulfilled before you feel you are a good son/daughter?

What has to be fulfilled before you feel you are a good parent?

What has to be fulfilled before you feel you are a good spouse?

What has to be fulfilled before you are a good brother/sister?

What has to be fulfilled before you are a good grandparent?

Are your rules in this area of life improving or decreasing the quality of your life?

Do you want to keep the rules in this area of your life or change them?

If you want to change them, go ahead and decide your new rules for this area right now.

Looking at your rules can be a pretty revealing affair. For some people it will suddenly make sense why, for example, they feel negative emotions more than positive ones or why they don't feel like a good parent or friend. Just because you don't feel like a good friend, it doesn't necessarily mean (even though it could) that you aren't.

This is where the exploration of your rules can be really valuable. By exploring your rules, you can determine whether you really believe you aren't a good friend or whether you have just set the criteria for being a good friend so high that you almost don't dare feel like a good friend unless you have saved someone's life several times within the same month.

If you really feel you aren't a good friend, then you can now take responsibility and do something about it. If you feel your criteria have just been too high, you can just change the rules by choosing new criteria.

**"When you create the rules of
the game, it is very easy to win."
—Mateo Tabatabai**

Transformation Exercise

Find the movie *Don Juan Demarco* (1994) with Johnny Depp and watch it. Even if you have watched this movie before, you should watch it again with all the new knowledge you have now acquired.

Make sure to really watch how the main character (Don Juan) uses his power as a meaning maker to interpret the world in his own unique way.

Also look for his rules for the different areas of life and see if you can spot places in the movie where he could have used his meaning-making skills in a more positive way in terms of his life quality. Don't miss this exercise, it will allow you to see many of the theories I have shared with you in action.

Your Power as a Meaning Maker

I clearly remember how I could sit for hours and play with my muscular action figures when I was a kid. I could play for hours just banging them into each other and making all sorts of sounds. I would build my own universe around such a simple thing and I disappear into this universe. It was like getting sucked into a black hole and entering a completely different world. It was my own beautiful illusion, an illusion that gave me a place where I could express all of my emotions, get caught up in these emotions, and surrender to these emotions.

I didn't care about people looking at me; I didn't even notice people looking at me because I was so caught up in the exploits my action figures were undertaking. Sometimes they would save a princess, other times they would save the planet, and when I felt really in my element, they were bad guys who wanted to ravage a city. To me they were alive, to me they were a part of the very universe I had created and I was now part of.

When I grew up I stopped playing with my action figures. I didn't stop because it was childish; I stopped because I realized that I could quadruple the fun by making the entire universe my playground instead.

Every single day of my life is play and art. Within my illusion all is well, people love each other, people are friendly and honest and LOVE to have fun. Within my illusion, paradise on Earth is no longer something you long for, but something you experience fully in each and every moment.

Within my illusion, you laugh and rejoice when life hits you hard, you laugh because it is all play anyway. Within my illusion, crying is not embarrassing, but one of the most beautiful and vulnerable things you can do.

I see people day in and day out longing for someone to come and rock their world, to shake the very foundation they are standing on and make them remember that they are ALIVE. People are caught in their robotic states in a constant state of worry about all the things they believe cause them pain.

Humans just want to play, laugh, and connect. But they also have fears, insecurities, and limiting beliefs they are not aware of.

This is holding them back! It is making them suffer, and all their life force is squeezed out of them by the iron grip of their so-called truth.

This is when we come into the picture. We play in our illusion and we send out an invitation to everyone on our path to join our play, rejoicing, and lightheartedness. If they don't want to play, great! We will transmute that energy of fear into more positivity for our world. If you want to play, thank you. Thank you for bringing your beauty and joining our dance.

Life is a dance, my friend, it is to be danced. Don't be the person who sits in the corner and thinks about when he should get up and dance. You can't be doing something if you are not already doing it, and you are supposed to be dancing.

Life is nothing but a dance, and you were born to dance. You sit and hope for someone to pull you into their dance. Maybe it happens, maybe it doesn't, but I can tell you this: life can be an incredible dance, and it is just waiting for you to get up from your chair and join the festivities.

> **"Let go of all that is no longer serving you and realize that an infinite power lies in your present moment."**
> —**Mateo Tabatabai**

CHAPTER 4
Becoming Aware of Your Limiting Beliefs

The only way you can ever change any of your beliefs is to first become aware of them. Without awareness of a given belief, you are going to be in a constant reaction state without even understanding why. When I want to discover hidden beliefs I am not yet aware of, I use two different methods. These two methods are not only extremely powerful but also very simple.

Even though these two methods are different ways of becoming aware of your limiting beliefs, they both have the same goal: weakening or eliminating your limiting beliefs through the power of awareness.

As I have talked about earlier, most of your limiting beliefs are only there because your mind thinks they are in some way serving you. Therefore, it is quite natural that your limiting beliefs lose a lot of their power once you become aware of them and realize they are the root of a lot of the suffering in your life.

The Methods

1. Self-Inquiry/Questioning

The first way I become aware of limiting beliefs is through self-inquiry. The way I do self-inquiry is to question whether a given belief is really serving me or not. Checking your rules for the different areas of your life (as we did in the last chapter) is one example of self-inquiry.

I will get into the specifics of self-inquiry at the end of this chapter so you can start using this method in all areas of your life. For now, however, I want to focus on the second method I use for discovering limiting beliefs.

2. Awareness

This method entails bringing your awareness to the present moment and focusing on whatever it is you are doing. It really doesn't matter what you are doing, just be present and observe any thoughts or emotions that suddenly come out of the nothingness.

I find it easier to become aware of the emotions I feel than the thoughts that come up. Since your beliefs and emotions are deeply connected, it really doesn't matter which one you notice, as they both make us aware of the same thing.

Examples of this:

Becoming aware of a thought:

You are preparing a presentation you have to make at work and you are fully present while doing so. Suddenly you notice a thought arise, "Hmm, I hope I don't screw it up tomorrow."

This is usually the expression of an underlying limiting belief. If you start questioning it and get to the root of it, you are almost guaranteed to find some pretty big limiting beliefs about failure, self-worth, your presentation skills, and other things.

Most people have "small" thoughts like these all the time, and they are so used to them that they just ignore them. This is why we need to be present so that we don't just ignore these thoughts or don't notice them at all. These so-called small thoughts have their origins in much larger limiting beliefs that you will never discover if you just ignore the small thoughts.

Becoming aware of an emotion:

You look at yourself in the mirror and suddenly feel a painful emotion. Instead of just ignoring this emotion, you need to immediately bring your attention to the present moment (if you are not already there) and explore it. Start going into it and find out if you missed any thoughts that are causing this emotion.

You might discover that just a few seconds prior to this emotion, you thought, "I knew I shouldn't have eaten that cupcake, I am starting to look fat again."

Ouch, is that really the kind of self-talk you want to engage in now that you know most of your thoughts are just self-fulfilling prophecies waiting to happen?

What Makes the Awareness Method So Powerful?

Most of the beliefs that are currently controlling your life are actually very easy to spot, if you are aware of whatever it is you are doing. The reason most people usually don't spot these beliefs is that they have become such a natural part of their everyday life they don't pay attention to them anymore.

This concept works in the same way as driving. When you first learned how to drive, you needed to be really focused and aware of all the things you were doing. Now you just get in the car, and suddenly you realize you have arrived at your desired location.

There is no longer a need for you to be aware of the things you are doing, since all the instructions for driving have been instilled deeply in your muscle memory and it has become an unconscious activity.

When our mind "knows" something, it doesn't see the need to focus a lot of attention on it anymore. If you have had certain beliefs for a long period of time, you have grown so accustomed to their running your life that you don't even register them anymore.

This is great if all your beliefs are completely empowering and continuously improving the quality of your life. In my experience, however, everyone, and that includes some of the most successful people in the world, has beliefs they can change or tweak in order to improve the quality of their lives.

Most people have a lot of negative and self-defeating beliefs they are completely unaware of, and because self-mastery is a continuous process and not a destination, there are always positive changes to make.

We are constantly thinking the same thoughts and entertaining the same beliefs. As a result, we are manifesting the same experience of life again and again. Studies show that up to 90% of what we say, think, and do is what we said, thought, and did the day before.

It is pretty easy to see that constantly entertaining the same limiting beliefs isn't the best idea when our mind is designed to focus on and reinforce any beliefs we have.

The only way to stop this vicious cycle is through the power of awareness. When you bring awareness to situations where you are usually unaware, you are telling your mind that even though it thinks it knows a given situation, you still need its complete attention and focus.

When you are fully present with whatever it is you are doing, something interesting happens. When you are present, you are literally going to see your limiting beliefs as they come out of nowhere and try to take control of your behavior.

The more awareness you bring to the present moment, the more you will realize there are all sorts of negative beliefs running in the background. These are the programs you don't usually notice because you are either in the past or the future.

> **"Let us not look back in anger**
> **or forward in fear, but around in**
> **awareness."**
> **—James Thurber**

Most of us are constantly in the past or the future, and we don't even realize how little time we actually spend in the present.

Some examples of this:

- We visit a beautiful place and are so busy taking pictures to show our friends that we completely miss the experience of the actual location we are photographing.

- We have long conversations while being completely unaware of the actual conversation; instead, we are thinking about what we are going to do later.

- We lie in bed after a long day and instead of just being there, we are busy planning what we are going to do the next day, despite the fact that we have been looking forward to lying in bed all day long.

- We finally get the promotion we have been waiting on for so long and instead of enjoying the raise we just got, we start worrying about what might happen if we don't live up to the new job description.

- After justifying why we really deserve to eat a meal of junk food, we finally decide to go for it. Instead of just enjoying it, however, we are busy thinking about how many calories we need to burn as a result of eating this meal.

- We sit and meditate, and instead of just sitting in silence, we are thinking about when we will reach a calm and relaxed state of mind.

When I talk of the present moment, some people get a little guarded because they have this notion that presence is an advanced skill reserved for only the most spiritual people.

Being present has nothing to do with spirituality, it is a basic life skill you need to practice and master if you want to enjoy a high quality of life. Some of our best memories are of when we were completely present and focusing fully on what we were doing.

Being present in those moments came completely naturally and wasn't something we could only do because we had decades of meditation practice.

If you don't bring awareness to your present moment, you will go through life never truly experiencing anything because you are always caught up in what the next experience is going to be. When we are not aware of the present moment, we are just living in constant reaction to the external world.

It is almost like you hit the autopilot switch because you need to disappear into the past or the future for a while. There are also people who have completely forgotten there is such a thing as the autopilot switch and that they have had it on for a few years now. I can think of at least a couple of women I have met who suspected this is where their husbands were stuck.

How many times have you suddenly realized you haven't really been present and that you spent the last 5 minutes of your time in some imaginary construct of the mind? Just go to a public place and take a look at people. It is truly surreal to see how often it is just a body sitting there, while the "owner" has taken a trip somewhere entirely different.

Most people view trance as some powerful trick of the evil guy with the monocle. They don't realize their life is a constant state of trance, with small moments of presence in between.

Don't you remember how exciting it was when you first met your spouse? How nervous or giggly you could get? How alive you could feel when you were together? How time could just fly?

What happened? The difference lies in the amount of awareness you are bringing to the relationship.

Have you ever gone on vacation with your spouse and suddenly felt like you were on your honeymoon again? Or felt they had really changed and they were not like you thought they were? This isn't because of the sun, the beach, and the delicious piña coladas.

It is because you suddenly have an excuse to be aware, because you are experiencing something "special" and new. When you are aware, you actually see the person in front of you and turn off the autopilot switch.

Being present with what you are doing is not something you can only do if you live a life that is constantly filled with "special" events. You can be present through the simple act of bringing quality to the normal things you do.

- Awareness in your everyday life can be something as simple as enjoying the water you drink.

- Really feeling it when you tell someone that you love him or her.

- Actually listening to the other person and trying to understand where they are coming from.

- Enjoying your breakfast like you just got out of prison and you haven't had a proper meal for 30 years.

- How about having sex like you are the greatest lover in the world and all you want to do is connect with your significant other?

Awareness is the backbone of living a life you enjoy, a life that isn't so automatic that you have to live in the future or the past in order to feel alive. When you start becoming more aware in your life, you start to understand that you are indeed in control of your thoughts, emotions, and behavior.

The number one comment I always hear when I talk about awareness is, "If I am supposed to be in the present moment constantly, I can never plan anything, and that is completely impractical." Being aware of the present moment has nothing to do with not planning what you are going to do in the future.

As of writing this, I have been traveling the world for almost 4 years, and as you can imagine, this would be pretty hard to do if I couldn't plan ahead.

Being aware of the present moment simply means you never believe the illusion that the future is going to be better than what is going on right now.

Plan, dream, and organize all you want; just don't start believing that what you have planned for the future is going to be any better than your current moment. You are going to be in the present moment your entire life. If you are focusing on how good the future (that really doesn't exist) is going to be, you are just running on the hamster wheel hoping to get somewhere.

Life is right now, in this glorious moment right in front of you. I believe that if you are not allowing yourself to be happy right NOW, nothing external in the future is going to change that permanently.

In fact, there was a very interesting study done by Phillip Brickman, Dan Coates, and Ronnie Janoff-Bulman. These researchers studied both lottery winners and individuals who had become paralyzed to determine if winning the lottery made them happier or if sustaining an injury made them less happy.

What they found was that immediately after either event, levels of happiness were higher (lottery winners) or lower (physically injured), and that after 8 weeks or less, people returned to the level of happiness they had before the event!

This type of research shows us that we adapt to both "good" and "bad" external changes very quickly and often return to our old level of happiness within just a couple of weeks.

> **"Happiness is a skill, not an acquisition."**
> **—Barbara De Angelis**

There is always going to be something else you want to achieve in life, and some teachers say you need to kill this desire in order to end your suffering. I believe our desire is one of the most powerful tools in our arsenal and it drives and fuels us to create and innovate.

I am not asking you to sit in the full lotus all day because nothing out there is worth achieving. I am simply saying that it is a pity to use a future achievement as an excuse not to enjoy the current moment and the journey towards a given goal. By becoming aware of the present moment, you will start living life where it always happens.

Full Acceptance of Whatever Comes Up

This is probably the most important step of the awareness method. If you don't understand it, it is not going to be a lot of fun to uncover your limiting beliefs. You need to make absolutely sure you have full acceptance for whatever thoughts or emotions come up during this process regardless of how negative you perceive them to be.

My definition of acceptance:

The recognition that something is taking place in this current moment. Acceptance doesn't mean you like or dislike whatever is taking place; it simply means that you non-judgmentally recognize it is there.

My definition of resistance:

Resisting the fact that something is taking place and trying to run away from the experience you are having.

If you feel emotions and thoughts of insecurity, jealousy, hate, sadness, or whatever coming up while using the awareness method, it is important that you just watch them with full acceptance and see if they have anything of value to tell you.

Don't start judging these emotions and trying to push them away because they make you feel uncomfortable; doing this will only make the suffering worse. I know it seems counterintuitive to just accept that these emotions and thoughts are there, but it works 100% of the time.

As I have mentioned earlier, the problem is never the emotion itself, but the context in which the emotion and beliefs are being utilized. If you don't fully accept that a certain emotion or thought is there, you are going to resist it. When you resist it, you are going to judge, blame, or feel guilty.

This means that in your effort to get rid of the emotion of jealousy, you add another layer, shame over the fact that you are jealous. It means that in your effort to get rid of the thought of worthlessness, you add a layer of blame.

A typical example of using your thoughts and emotions in the wrong context is when someone eats something they are not supposed to eat. They then feel guilty over the fact that they couldn't restrain themselves.

Instead of accepting the emotion of guilt is there and that it might even have something valuable to tell them (for instance, that a certain type of food is not good for their health), they start resisting it. They resist the emotion of guilt by starting a pattern of blame and negative self-talk. This leads to sadness, and in their effort to hide (resist) the sadness, they eat even more.

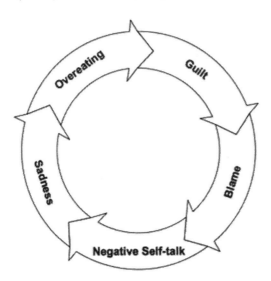

They could have avoided this whole cycle if they had just accepted that the feeling of guilt has arisen in them and checked whether it has something valuable to tell them. Sometimes the emotion is really trying to give you some valuable information.

For example, you feel guilty because you procrastinated about not going to the gym for the 10th time in a row or you fear going into a dangerous neighborhood at night. In a scenario such as fear of a dangerous neighborhood, the emotion of fear is probably adding value to your life and improving your survival chances by protecting you.

Other times the emotion doesn't have anything of value to tell you. It is only there because you have a belief that is not constructive to the quality of your life. Examples of this are being ashamed of your sexuality or fearing public speaking.

When the emotion has nothing of value to offer you, it is time for some self-inquiry. The self-inquiry will show you the underlying beliefs you have created that are making you feel a given emotion in a context where it is not really improving the quality of your life.

In either case, you never judge or resist the emotion. The emotion or thought is only there because of the underlying beliefs you have created. You need to accept the symptom so you can get to the root of things and start creating change.

A common objection I get when I talk about full acceptance of whatever emotions and thoughts come up is, "But I don't want to accept that I have these thoughts and emotions that are causing me all this pain, I can't live with that!"

Bringing acceptance to whatever comes up in the present moment is very different than not doing anything about it. You have to understand that the first thing you need to do is to be able to see an emotion or thought for what it is, without getting sucked into its story.

As demonstrated in the overeating example, you are going to stir up the mud even more by trying to resist it, and before you know it, you don't even know what you are trying to resist anymore. Only once you have accepted that a thought or emotion is there can you start questioning its validity and finding the underlying reason.

Full acceptance of the current moment is definitely not about being passive and sticking your head in the sand. Acceptance of the current moment is all about making a logical and clear-headed decision, something you can only do when you fully recognize where you currently are and where you want to go. If you don't want to recognize and accept where you currently are, you are not going to be going anywhere better.

A couple of years ago I started a company and put a lot of time and effort into getting it up and running. For 6 months straight I was doing 8 to 12 hours of daily work while I was also studying to become an engineer.

In this period of my life I would typically get 4 to 5 hours of sleep. I would say no to almost all social engagements because I was so passionate about getting my business up and running. Around the 4-month mark I had started getting some results, and by the 6-month mark, things were looking really good in terms of profit margins.

By this time I had hired a couple of employees to work for me so I could ease up on the work and take some much-needed relaxation time.

Literally one week later a perceived tragedy struck, and my entire business model got outdated. I tried to resist what had happened for a couple of days by thinking about how unfair it was and how I would never start a company again.

After a couple of days, I decided it was time to be mature and fully accepted what I was experiencing. When I stopped resisting what had happened, I finally had enough resources to figure out what the next step was going to be.

Things that are out of our control happen all the time. Whether we resist them or accept them really doesn't change the fact that they have now become a part of our experience in the present moment. Resisting will confuse you and give you additional suffering. Full acceptance will allow you to step out of the situation and figure out the best way to proceed.

I have learned many things that really improved the quality of my life by leaps and bounds. Of all the things I have learned, however, one of the most powerful lessons was that I have the power to accept ANYTHING that happens in my life.

Once I really understood this on an emotional level, I knew that nothing could ever hurt me in life, and even if it did, I had the ability to accept the situation and the hurt.

I am going to share a secret with you: This power is not reserved for all the Mateos in the world. I am going to tell you another secret: YOU possess this power too.

If you can take away just one thing from this book, this is definitely the realization to go for. If you do, you can say goodbye to the majority of your fear and worry. There is nothing to fear or worry about when you know you have the ability to accept whatever might happen in the future.

"Of course there is not a formula for success except, perhaps, an unconditional acceptance of life and what it brings."
—**Arthur Rubinstein**

The Awareness Method in Practical Terms

Being present is not an advanced technique, and anyone can do it. All you have to do is put your focus on what you are actually doing and, every time your mind wanders, gently bring your attention back.

Even though this method can be used in all situations, I find it is particularly powerful in public places and in interactions with other people. This is usually where our limiting beliefs go really crazy and we make all sorts of negative interpretations.

Therefore, you can find a lot of limiting beliefs by simply being present when you interact with people. Presence in interaction with people is done by bringing your full attention to the interaction and watching, listening, and feeling as much as you can.

Make sure to really listen not only to what the other person is saying, but also to the silence between their words. Likewise, be completely aware of your own words and the silence between them when you respond.

If any beliefs or emotions that are not constructive to your life (cause you suffering) suddenly come up, simply accept that they are there and make a mental note of them so you can get to the bottom of them as soon as you are alone.

In the beginning it can feel challenging to maintain awareness of the present moment. Like everything else in life, however, it is only a challenge until it becomes easy.

The more you practice, the easier it is going to become. The most important thing is to view this whole process as play and not get frustrated when your attention wanders off and you start daydreaming, something that can happen a lot in the beginning.

Exercise to get started with the awareness method

Try being present in as many interactions as you can for a whole day. Really be present with your spouse, children, parents, friends, and even complete strangers. Every single interaction in our life is important, even the ones that we typically view as insignificant, for example, talking to the cashier at the grocery store or signing for a delivery from the UPS guy.

Bring awareness to every single one of your interactions for one day and see what you notice. You can do this by really listening and connecting to the person you are interacting with. By doing this, you will become aware of the limiting thoughts and emotions that suddenly come up and try to take over.

Alternative way to be present in your interactions

Another fun way to keep your focus on the interactions is to find traits in people that you hadn't noticed about them before. This includes not only their appearance, but also their personality. To do this, you automatically have to be present and really listen to what they are saying.

It is such an amazing experience when you find new things about people you have known for years. You suddenly see that your mom, dad, husband/wife, children, and friends have their own internal universes and that they have their own joys and challenges in life.

You see them for the human beings they are in that moment instead of just using the preconceived notions you have of them. This bonus exercise is all about sensitivity to others. If you can make it a regular part of your everyday life, you will connect with people in a way you have never connected before.

I would like you to start with either one of the above-mentioned exercises as an introduction to using the awareness method to discover limiting beliefs. With practice, you will start becoming more aware of your thoughts and emotions even without trying. You will always have your hands full with new beliefs you can optimize and tweak if you wish to do so.

Now that you know how to become aware of the thoughts and emotions that are decreasing the quality of your life, we need to move to the next step. The next step is the self-inquiry part, where you get to the root of your beliefs and see whether you want to keep them or not.

Self-Inquiry

Self-inquiry is the method of going inside yourself and questioning the validity of a given belief. When you find beliefs that are not serving you, you can use self-inquiry to see why you have that belief.

Likewise, if you suddenly feel negative emotions, you can use the self-inquiry method to figure out what caused that specific emotion and then start getting to the root of it. The importance of questioning the things you believe in lies in the fact that you often realize your beliefs are formed on completely arbitrary "truths."

An example of this is the man who believes all women are manipulative and evil, just because his mom took advantage of his dad.

Once you see how random the structure of some of your beliefs can be and that they really don't make any sense, they automatically lose a lot of their power because you realize they have no solid foundation.

Some good questions to use when doing self-inquiry:

- Why do I believe this?

- Do I know with absolute certainty that this is true?

- How do I know this?

- Do I have permission to change this belief?

- Is this belief enhancing or decreasing the quality of my life?

- Why do I feel this way?

- What secondary benefits am I getting from believing this?

Example of self-inquiry for an emotion:

Let's say you run into an old classmate and decide to have a cup of coffee with her and catch up. As you sit in the café, your conversation goes in the direction of work, and she mentions that she has started her own business. She says, "Last year I decided to start my own business, and it has become a huge success. What do you do for work?"

Let's say that you are a stay-at-home mom, and this is something you always thought you were really proud of. The moment you go to answer, you suddenly notice a negative emotion, however. You say, "Ahh, I don't really work right now, I am just a stay-at-home mom."

By using the awareness method and bringing presence to your feelings (if you weren't already present), you notice that the emotion you felt was embarrassment or not being good enough. You take note of this emotion and when it occurred so you can get to the bottom of it when you are alone.

When your interaction is done, it is time to figure out what was really going on in your mind, to find the belief that caused the feeling of not being good enough. This is when we use self-inquiry to get to the root of things.

- Why did I feel like I was not good enough when I said I was a stay-at-home mom? *Because she has become successful and she has her own company.*

- Do I enjoy being a stay-at-home mom and spending time with my children? *Yes, of course.*

- Then why did I feel like I wasn't good enough? *Well, because she is going to think that I am not successful.*

- Why is it important to me that she think I am successful? *Because I don't want her to think I am just wasting my life.*

- Is spending time with my children wasting my life? *NO, of course not.*

- Then why is it important that she think I am successful? *Because I don't want her to think I just gave up on my other dreams.*

- Why does it matter what she thinks of me? *Because I want people to like me.*

- Why do I want people to like me? *Because that gives me a really nice feeling and I don't like it if someone thinks ill of me.*

- Why don't I like it if someone thinks ill of me? *Hmm . . . Well, I guess because that would mean that I am not good enough.*

- Is my worth determined by what other people think of me? *Well, not really. But as a kid I learned that it is really important that others like you, and this has always stuck with me.*

- Do I know with absolute certainty that this belief is true? *No.*

- Is this belief improving the quality of my life or not? *It is not really improving my life because it is draining to constantly need to have everyone like you.*

- Am I willing to change this belief? *Absolutely.*

Example of self-inquiry for a thought:

You visit your parents, and after dinner, you have a conversation with your father. He gives you some pointers or a lecture on how you should raise your child.

Dad: "I have noticed that you don't really teach Brian any real discipline. You really have to show kids who the boss is or else they will walk all over you."

As you start to respond, you suddenly become aware of the thought "Yeah right, like you have any idea how to raise a child."

Instead of just ignoring this thought like most people do, you use the awareness method to note that this thought came up so you can start the questioning process once you get home.

- Why did I have that thought? Haven't my parents given me a good upbringing? *Of course they have . . . But there were times when I felt my emotions were ignored and I was treated unfairly.*

- When was this? *There was one time when my father scolded me because I was running around in the house and I broke a vase by accident. For some reason I remember this event very clearly.*

- Why was this unfair? *Because I never got the chance to explain myself and he told me that I should just shut it.*

- How did that make me feel? *Angry. I remember that I punched the wall really hard when I got back in my room.*

- How did I feel about this anger? *I felt I was helpless and couldn't do anything. He had the last word because he was the boss, and it really didn't matter what I felt about the situation.*

- How did this helplessness make me feel? *I didn't like it one bit, that's what . . . Damn it, I think this is why I always get really angry if there is an authority figure that tries to tell me what to do.*

- What does it mean if someone tells me what to do? *That they are bossing me around and they are not willing to hear my side of the story (pretty negative meaning to create).*

- Do I know this to be absolutely true? *No, not really.*

- Could it be that they are just trying to tell me a better way to do things (much more positive meaning)? *I guess so, yeah.*

- Is this belief improving the quality of my life? *Not really.*

- Am I willing to try out a new belief instead? *Yes.*

As you can see, the self-inquiry method is pretty much identical whether you notice an emotion or a belief. In both cases you are stepping backwards to get to the underlying belief that is the root of the thought or emotion you become aware of.

When you finally get to the root of it, you need to ask yourself whether you are willing to change the limiting belief or not. By doing this, you are committing yourself to change, and two things will happen: It will become easier to change the belief, and it will become easier to notice it if that belief creeps up and tries to take control again.

The method of self-inquiry requires you to be patient and willing to just flow with the energy and see where the questioning process takes you. At the same time, it is important that you be ruthless and see yourself as a samurai who is slashing through illusion after illusion until you get to the root of your suffering.

Sometimes you end in some truly surprising places. I have had many clients who are absolutely blown away when they find the real reasons for why they do the things they do.

- Some think that the problem is lack of willpower, when in reality it is a deep sense of worthlessness.

- Some think their body is just prone to anger fits, when in reality it is all caused by the belief that humiliation is the worst thing that can happen to you.

- Some people are convinced they had a tough upbringing (which might be true) and then find out they are only focusing on that as a reason for not taking responsibility for their life right now. Underlying belief: I am just meant to have a tough life and my upbringing is proof of that.

Some pointers for performing self-inquiry

Letting the questions direct you

It is important that you not be biased and already "know" what is causing a given emotion or thought beforehand. Be present with the inquiry process and see where it takes you. In other words, be willing to flow with the questions.

If you suddenly see that your questioning is going in a completely different direction than you had first expected, then by all means go for it and see where it takes you.

Honesty

You need to be honest with yourself. This is absolutely crucial if you want to get anything out of your self-inquiry. If you are not honest, you are just wasting your time. There might be some things you fear accepting about yourself. This is where you need to prioritize and choose whether you want stay in the comfort of keeping your old limiting beliefs intact or actually want to improve the quality of your life.

Should Versus Reality

Don't answer the questions with what you believe you SHOULD feel. Answer the questions with what you REALLY feel. This can be frightening. However, you need to trust that even though honesty might cause you some pain in the moment, it is going to improve the quality of your life by leaps and bounds.

Being honest is the only way you can let go of the lies and illusions you have been carrying around for such a long time. It takes huge amounts of energy to maintain a façade between yourself and others day in and day out.

Details are king

It is important to answer the questions as specifically as you can. Really dig deep and answer your self-inquiry questions with as much detail as you possibly can. Even though general answers can help, you are going to have much more profound results by being as specific as you can.

You are the expert

If you feel like you have hit a dead end, feel free to guess what you think the answer to the question is. Often you will find that your guesses are going to be pretty accurate, and more importantly, they will allow you to move forward in your exploration of your inner world.

Remember that you are the expert when it comes to you. I can sit here and pretend to be the expert all I want, but nobody knows you better than you do. When it comes to matters of you, you are the leading consultant in the world, and it is important that you trust your inner knowing.

Partnering

For many people, it is much easier to get someone else to do the questioning. If you have someone you can really trust, you can ask them whether they want to help you. One important note: The person questioning you should never have the goal of "fixing" anything or start interpreting why you believe what you believe.

Exploring, Not Fixing

This process is not about fixing anything. It is simply about exploring the beliefs of your mind and seeing how your inner world is operating. If you happen to find beliefs and meanings that are not improving the quality of your life, by all means go ahead and change them.

You shouldn't have the expectation of finding something to fix. Your mind is perfect just as it is and doesn't need fixing; sometimes it is just fun to have a nice tune-up of some of the old beliefs that are no longer serving you.

Give yourself permission to get it completely wrong

It is completely fine if you don't have any major realizations on the first couple of tries. Don't beat yourself up over it. Just make a note of the given emotion or thought that you originally became aware of and try to come back later to double-check if there is anything negative lurking underneath the surface.

Don't judge or blame

By now this goes without saying. Don't judge or blame the things you learn about yourself when you are exploring. Accept whatever you find and continue until you get to the root of the problem. Once there, you can make a logical decision about whether or not a given belief is valuable to your life.

You now know the theory behind bringing awareness into your life and spotting limiting beliefs and emotions that are out of context. You also know how to explore and get to the root of your beliefs through self-inquiry and questioning.

These two methods alone will greatly weaken the structures of your existing limiting beliefs or completely eliminate them from your life by helping you realize that a given belief is no longer serving you. Once you realize that a belief is no longer valuable for you, it is time to install a new and more empowering belief instead, and this is where we use the Belief Changer.

> **"Every man takes the limits of his own field of vision for the limits of the world."**
> **—Arthur Schopenhauer**

113

The Belief Changer

The belief changer is an essential tool when it comes to taking back control of your life. You can use the belief changer to install any new beliefs you think would be constructive to the quality of your life.

The belief changer is a very powerful tool, and therefore it is important that you first check whether a given belief is truly healthy for your life or not before installing it.

Even though the belief "Winning isn't everything, it's the only thing" might be extremely productive to some people, it can ruin the lives of others because they will become complete workaholics who have no time for their family. Therefore, you need to make sure that a belief is truly positive to the quality of your life before installing it.

Where do you find empowering beliefs?

I find my beliefs in two different ways. Either I create whatever belief I want to have from scratch, or I come across someone else's belief that I really like. I often find a lot of great new beliefs by reading the work of role models who have succeeded in the areas of life that I want to succeed in. Another great way to find really empowering beliefs is to go through quotes and find the ones that really resonate with you.

If you choose to adopt another person's beliefs, it is important that you make sure this person is actually getting the results you want in life.

If, for example, you want to become financially independent, it is probably not going to be very beneficial for you to study the beliefs of someone who is not yet financially free. Sure, this person might have some great ideas, but if his ideas are so good, then why isn't he already financially free?

Installing the belief into your system

When you have a belief that is both powerful and healthy for your life, it is time to start the installation process. There are many different ways in which you can install a belief into your system. Most of the methods have one thing in common: you have to immerse yourself in the new belief and keep reinforcing it until it becomes a natural part of you.

All the beliefs you currently have were learned through constant reinforcement. Therefore, we are just mimicking the natural function of the mind to install new and more empowering beliefs.

The two-step process I am now going to share with you is one way to install new beliefs, and it is the most powerful method I have come across to this day.

The Belief Changer consists of two steps: priming and reinforcing. You prime your mind to a given belief by doing affirmations. Your affirmations will introduce a new belief into the circuit of your mind. Once a belief is introduced to the mind, you can then start the real installation by finding evidence for it (reinforcement).

Step 1. Affirmations

The first thing you have to understand is that affirmations are not very effective if you do them like most people do them. Most people just mumble their affirmations and get them over with as quickly as possible.

Installing a new belief is all about full involvement. You need to be willing to completely immerse yourself in the time period when you do your affirmations.

It is essential that you use as much of your physiology and emotion as you possibly can when doing your affirmations. Extensive research in this area clearly shows that memories and beliefs are also stored within our body.

Therefore, it is important that you get your body as involved as you can when doing your affirmations. I usually stand in front of a mirror and put the maximum amount of my tonality, emotions, and body gestures into the affirmations.

The next mistake people make when doing affirmations is that they try to install beliefs like "I am really wealthy" or "I am really fit." These affirmations are beliefs that your mind views as complete lies, and as soon as your mind hears them, it is going to call your bluff and give you thousands of reasons for why you are neither wealthy nor fit.

When you try to install a belief like "I am a millionaire" when you really are not, you are trying to fight your mind. We need to work with our mind and transcend its perceived limitations instead of fighting it.

If you want the maximum benefit from your affirmations, you need to use beliefs that you actually believe are true on an intellectual level. When I say this, people always ask me, "But what if I am really not wealthy?"

We need to think a little outside the box here. By doing so we can find a lot of beliefs that can help us become wealthy and at the same time are principles/beliefs that your mind can perceive to be true on an intellectual level.

Some examples of these kinds of beliefs:

- It is a lot easier to become wealthy if you are taking massive action towards your goals.

- There are three key factors involved in becoming wealthy: persistence, patience, and discipline.

- Being wealthy allows you to help others who are in need.

- The person who can continuously push himself forward, even when the effort gets painful, will always reach his goal.

Installing these principles in your mind is going to be a lot easier than claiming "I am a millionaire" when every cell in your body is screaming that you are not. Your mind is going to have a lot less resistance to installing these kinds of beliefs because it can see the "logic" in them.

Installing such beliefs is going to change your behavior because you are giving a new set of rules to your mind for how it needs to operate. If, for example, you install the belief "It is a lot easier to become wealthy if you are taking massive action towards your goals," your mind is going to start following this rule and push you towards taking action.

The next step is to start doing the actual affirmations, and this is the way you are going to do it:

I believe that (insert the belief you have chosen).

From this day forward I will (insert the belief you have chosen).

An example of your affirmation could be:

- **I believe that** it is a lot easier to become wealthy if you are taking massive action towards your goals.

- **From this day forward I will** take massive action towards my goals because I know that it is a lot easier to become wealthy when I am doing so.

117

I am going to repeat this because it is extremely important in terms of the effectiveness of your affirmations: You really need to get your body, voice, and emotions involved in the process.

When you say "I believe x," you need to use the same convinced body language, emotions, and tonality that you would use if you were really sure of something.

The same applies when you say "From this day forward I will . . ." You need to use the same body language, emotions, and tonality you would use when you are absolutely committed to something.

Remember that the key to installing a new belief is to immerse yourself. Therefore, you need to do your affirmations on a daily basis until you get to the point where you know a belief is now installed.

You know you have reached this point when you just start acting on this belief without thinking about it. It can take days, weeks, and even months to reach this point.

You have to remember the big picture and understand that just one empowering belief can completely change the quality and direction of your life.

If you remember the idea of the leverage point, you will also remember how one single belief is going to affect tens or even hundreds of other beliefs because of the interconnectedness of our beliefs.

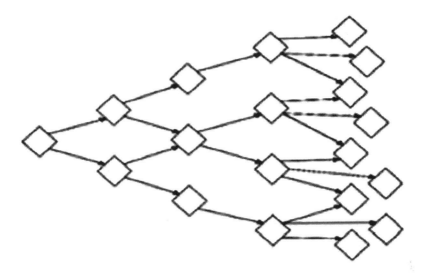

For this reason, it is definitely worth the effort to install new beliefs. Installing just five empowering beliefs a year has the potential to create RADICAL shifts. I almost quadrupled my annual income in 8 months when I spent about 10 minutes a day installing new empowering beliefs. On top of this, I am getting literally hundreds of other tangible as well as intangible benefits in my life that are a direct result of my belief installations.

I usually spend 2 to 5 minutes on each belief and then I move on to the next one. I suggest that you start with one to three beliefs and make your affirmations a daily habit. This is a much better idea than trying to install 50 beliefs at once and completely overwhelming yourself.

Last but not least, I want you to view your affirmations as something fun. When you really get your body, emotions, and tonality involved, it will actually be quite entertaining. Once you really start getting into it, you will feel an energy and power boost that can last throughout the day every time you do your affirmations.

Step 2. Reinforcing the Newly Introduced Belief

The affirmations are the first part of the process. The second part of the process is about reinforcing the belief you have just introduced to your mind. This part of the belief changer is really easy and entails looking for evidence that can support your new belief.

Just become aware of whatever evidence you can find to support this new belief and collect as much of it as possible. I want you to see yourself as a defense attorney who needs to do his best to prove that the new belief is really true.

It doesn't matter how "out there" or ridiculous your reasoning seems, just as long as it is supporting your new belief. It doesn't matter how ridiculous or "real" the evidence is because a lot of your existing beliefs are built on random evidence anyway.

Example:

Let's use the belief that "The person who can continuously push himself forward even when the effort gets painful will always reach his goal" in this example.

Evidence for your new belief:

• Most really successful athletes reach their goals because they are willing to continually push themselves forward.

• My most successful ventures in life have always been a result of going the extra mile when others weren't willing to do so.

• When I think about it, the only difference I can find between the people that are massively successful and the ones that live regular lives is that the successful group move forward even when the effort gets painful.

Let's assume this is the evidence you found right off the bat. Here are some examples of evidence you could find for your new belief in your everyday life:

- You see an old man who continually walks forward towards his goal of reaching the supermarket even though the effort is "painful."

- You see a musician who is playing music at the subway station and continuing to do so even though the weather is cold and the effort has gotten painful. You find further evidence for your new belief by telling yourself that you absolutely know he is going to reach his goal because he is willing to continually push himself forward.

- You do one or two extra pushups even when you feel like quitting, and you just have this inner knowing that continually doing this will allow you to reach your fitness goals.

- When the usually annoying door-to-door salesman knocks on your door, you use it as an opportunity to remember that because he is continually moving forward, even when the effort gets painful, he is guaranteed to reach his goal of making a sale.

Make this a game in your everyday life and find as much evidence for your new beliefs as you possibly can. If you start with just one to three new beliefs, it is going to be a breeze to do this.

Most people think it is hard to find evidence for a given belief, but they soon realize the power of the reticular activating system when they actually go out and try. Doing this is very powerful, and once you get the hang of it, you will be amazed at the amount of evidence you can effortlessly find for any new belief.

The affirmation introduces the new belief to your mind, and the search for evidence reinforces that new belief by mimicking what the mind usually does without our interference. The only difference is that this time, we are choosing what we want to find evidence for, and this is what free will is all about!

You can use the evidence game in two ways, positive and negative.

1. Positive

The positive evidence finder is the method I have just introduced to you, and it is an essential part of installing a new belief into your system.

I am also going to give you a bonus method that you can use at times when you want to *eliminate* a limiting belief.

2. Negative

The negative evidence finder consists of finding evidence for why a negative belief you have is not true. This method can be used to weaken and eliminate beliefs that you no longer want to have.

If, for example, you believe that it is impossible to get out of depression, you will play the negative evidence game by finding as much proof as possible that points to the contrary.

Go out and meet people who used to be depressed and overcame it, go online and find success stories, ask your doctors to tell you stories about people who overcame depression.

If someone starts giving you evidence for why it is hard to get out of depression, just understand that it might be hard according to that person's beliefs and realize that their beliefs don't have anything to do with your beliefs unless you allow them to.

This method works great when you do self-inquiry and find a limiting belief you have a hard time letting go of. When this happens, you simply start the process of finding as much evidence as you can for why that given limiting belief isn't true.

Both the negative and the positive evidence finder are extremely Powerful, and their power lies in the fact that this is what your mind will do on its own anyway. I used to be a meat eater, and as a pretty serious natural bodybuilder, I used to eat 1 to 2 pounds of beef, fish, or chicken every single day. I clearly remember how I would playfully tease vegetarians and tell them that real men needed their meat. I really believed this, and I didn't think I could be as strong if I didn't eat meat.

On top of this, it seemed like every vegetarian man I met was extremely skinny, and this was a constant reinforcement of my belief that you need to eat meat if you want to be strong.

My mind was basically just using the negative evidence finder to show me the negatives of being a vegetarian and the positive evidence finder to show me the benefits of being a carnivore.

Today I am a vegetarian and I believe that this is the right choice for me. The only difference lies in the fact that over time my mind started using the evidence finder to show me the negatives of eating meat and the positives of eating a plant-based diet instead.

If you look at your own life, you will see that your beliefs have changed a lot over the last decade and you could never get yourself to do some of the things you did back then and vice versa. The only difference lies in the fact that your beliefs have changed through negative and positive reinforcement over the last decade.

The power of the evidence finder (both the negative and the positive) lies in the fact that it is something your mind already does naturally, and therefore it is very simple to use this system to your advantage.

The systems I have shared with you in this chapter can be used as an integrated unit very easily. All the methods are extremely practical and can be implemented in your life immediately without taking up a lot of time. These are not methods that should work in theory or just look good on paper.

These methods absolutely work, and I know this because I have used them in my own life for several years and still use them on a daily basis. Furthermore, I have helped hundreds of clients successfully change their beliefs with the help of these methods.

These methods are tested, and all the hard work has been done for you. All you need to do is put them to use and get the life-changing benefits of being in control of what beliefs you entertain in your life.

A summary of the methods

I use two methods to become aware of my limiting beliefs.

The first method is the awareness method, which I use by bringing my full attention to the present moment. This method is particularly useful when it comes to uncovering limiting beliefs in your day-to-day life.

A good time to use this method is when you are interacting with others or you are in a public place. The awareness method is going to give you a wide collection of other benefits that I have also discussed in this chapter.

The second method to uncover limiting beliefs is self-inquiry. You can use this method by questioning some of the areas of your life that you suspect are run by limiting beliefs (we will do this in chapter 6), or you can use it to get to the root of the negative thoughts/emotions that the awareness method allows you to discover.

When you become aware of, and question, your limiting beliefs, they automatically lose a lot of their power because your mind starts to realize that they are no longer serving you.

If you have a hard time getting rid of a limiting belief even though you have become aware of it and questioned it, it is time to use the negative evidence finder and start finding tons of evidence for why it is not necessarily true.

This last step is only necessary for some of the most stubborn limiting beliefs, and when used in conjunction with the other two methods, it is guaranteed to eliminate any limiting belief.

When I discover that I have a limiting belief in a given area, I immediately want to find some empowering beliefs in that area and install them into my system. This is when I get assistance from the belief changer.

The belief changer can also be used when you just feel inspired and want to install a lot of new and empowering beliefs.

It consists of two steps. Step one is through affirmations, which introduce the new belief to the mind. Step two is reinforcement of the new belief by consistently finding evidence that supports it.

It is important that you install beliefs that you actually think are true on an intellectual level in order to avoid major resistance from your mind. It is also crucial that you use as much of your body, voice, and emotions as you possibly can when doing your affirmations.

Affirmations are done in two forms:

I believe that (insert the belief you have chosen).

From this day forward I will (insert the belief you have chosen).

You should do your affirmations on a daily basis until you start acting on the specific beliefs in your everyday life without thinking about it. Step two is when you find evidence for why your new beliefs are true.

This should be a game you do in your everyday life, and it is an important part of the installation process. The more evidence you find, the faster a given belief is going to be installed.

You continue finding evidence for the beliefs you are trying to install until the finding of evidence becomes an unconscious process (just as it is with all of your existing beliefs).

This method is guaranteed to work if you put in the little work needed. The two awareness methods go hand in hand with the belief changer. Implementing these techniques into your life can be a very natural process that doesn't take a lot of time.

By bringing awareness into your life, you will start having a completely different experience of life. The simplest things can become the greatest joys, and each moment is another chance to get a glimpse into the truly incredible experience we have been blessed with.

You will start to see your illusions for what they are, and one by one, your limiting beliefs will lose a lot of their power. Once you use the power of awareness to see these previously hidden agents of control, you will start to question them, and this questioning will eventually set you free.

I completely appreciate that you might not be ready to let go of some of your limiting beliefs yet, and I am not asking you to do so. There is no right or wrong in life, and therefore I would never ask you to change anything. You are absolutely perfect just as you are.

I am simply asking you to bring awareness to your experience so you yourself can start choosing the beliefs that are running your life. I am simply asking you to experience life more on your own terms.

When you choose the beliefs you want to entertain, you have started the process of designing your life experience. When you are in control of your beliefs, you no longer set goals and hope that they will someday come true; you simply decide what you want and design your beliefs so as to almost guarantee that you are going to get to your chosen destination.

> "Nobody can go back and start
> a new beginning, but anyone
> can start today and make a new
> ending."
> —Maria Robinson

CHAPTER 5
Habits That Ruin Lives

Before we get to the deep exploration of your beliefs in the next chapter, we need to deal with some of the concepts that typically hold people back.

It is key that we deal with these concepts before moving on. If you are not aware of these concepts, it becomes a lot harder to get to the root of your beliefs.

Blame

Most humans are blaming either something or someone for their current life situation. Often they have been doing it for such a long time that they are not really aware of it anymore.

Blame is so accepted in our society because people live under the false notion that the external world has way more power than it really has.

If you don't understand your internal power to create whatever meaning you like, it is going to seem logical to blame an external event or person for the emotional states you are feeling.

Some typical examples of blame:

- People just don't show me the respect I deserve, and therefore it is hard to be myself around them.

- My boss is an idiot and that is why he is not promoting me. I am sure he has something personal against me.

- It is hard for me to succeed because I had a tough upbringing. My parents beat me, taught me limiting beliefs, and did everything in their power to ruin my life. How could I ever have a high quality of life after what happened?

- My wife left me and I got fired at the same time! Of course I am depressed, look at my life and how I am constantly struck by tragedy.

- I am just unlucky and nothing ever goes right. Every single time things start going in a positive direction, I manage to throw it all away. I just know that this is all caused by the fact that I don't have a high level of confidence. If I just had more confidence, my life would be a lot better.

- It's easy for him to say; he didn't experience all the hardships that I did. If he had walked a mile in my shoes he definitely wouldn't be going on and on about positivity and successful mindsets in life.

- Well, of course they didn't pick me for the job, I am too fat. If I were skinny like those other applicants, they would have definitely chosen me. It is so unfair that we live in a society that judges people based on their weight.

- I could be a really good father if it wasn't for my wife. She always turns the kids against me by being nice to them just after I have disciplined them.

I often see people mistake blame and weaknesses that can be improved for the same thing, even though there is a big difference between the two.

Blame: My low confidence is really holding me back. This is why I can't do X and Y.

Weakness that can be improved: My low confidence is really holding me back. I need to figure out how I can improve my confidence so I can connect more with my inner power.

Blame has one function and one function only: to deny responsibility of your present moment because it is too painful to realize you are in fact responsible for the hurt you are feeling.

People who are caught in the blame game constantly have external reasons for why they can't do things. They run these stories in their mind so often that they themselves start believing them.

What people don't see is that blame is a double-edged sword. On one side it will give you a justification for why you can't do what you really want to do. This gives you a comfort zone where you don't have to take responsibility for your current life situation. A lot of people like this feeling of comfort and having something tangible they can point to as an explanation for their decreased quality of life.

On the other side of the coin, however, blame will take away all of your personal power. The reason for this is simple: If something external really is the cause of your decreased life quality, then you don't really have the power to change it because the solution can only come externally.

Feelings of powerlessness are very often seen among people who constantly blame the external world. Power and freedom are deeply connected with taking responsibility. You can't be truly free if you are blaming others for the things you are, in reality, responsible for.

Even if you really feel that something happened to you that you were not responsible for, you need to realize that you are responsible for how you are feeling and reacting to that experience right now.

It is so much easier to blame someone else than it is to take responsibility for your thoughts and actions. Just because it is easier to do so doesn't mean that you are not paying a huge price when you play the blame game.

The price you pay when you blame others is that you give away all of your personal power and pretend to be a victim who can't do anything. Is this really your highest intention? Is this who you are?

Blaming others lowers not only your life quality, but also the life quality of your social circle. A study done by Larissa and Fast Tiedens of Stanford University showed how socially contagious blaming others really is. The study had 100 participants with an average age of 31.

The participants were split into two groups, each of which got a news clip containing a statement by Governor Arnold Schwarzenegger about a failure. In one statement the governor took full responsibility for the failure, and in the other he blamed special-interest groups.

Later in the study the participants had to write about an unrelated personal failure and explain the reason behind it. Participants who had read the clip in which the governor blamed the special-interest groups were twice as likely to blame someone else for their personal failure as the participants in the other group.

I once had a client who said one of the things he really wanted to overcome was his constant blaming of others. We had uncovered this propensity to blame just a few minutes earlier, and he really wanted to stop it after realizing how much it was affecting his life.

I told him about the study that I have just shared with you and saw him go quiet for a few moments, and it looked like he suddenly had an insight.

I patiently observed his reactions, and he looked at me and said, "Of course I have been blaming others so much, both my mom and dad are huge blamers and I must have picked it up from them." I just couldn't help myself and I started laughing. After a few seconds of confusion he put his hand on his forehead and said, "I'm doing it again, aren't I? I am blaming again!" and he too started laughing.

This is exactly what I am referring to when I say that blame has become such a natural part of most people's lives that they are not aware of it anymore. People who blame others often show signs of overgeneralized thinking and overuse of projections in addition to their blame.

Overgeneralized thinking is making exaggerated statements like "You are ALWAYS against me . . . You NEVER care about my opinion . . . I have to do ALL the work around here . . . You NEVER show me love and affection . . . ALL you do is make me feel like I am worthless."

Projections are a common defense mechanism in which a person will become negative about a trait, thought, or emotion in someone else that they want to deny in themselves. By blaming others for that trait, you can avoid seeing it in yourself.

Just listen to someone criticizing others and you will quickly see that the things they are judging about others are the same traits they themselves possess or are self-conscious about.

Some common projection scenarios:

- People who are absolute control freaks criticize someone else for being too domineering and controlling.

- You are verbally outsmarted in an argument and say, "You are just so stupid, you don't get it."

- The wife who never listens to her husband and then yells at him because he never listens to her.

- Someone who feels worthless will constantly make fun of others and try to make them feel worthless.

- Someone who is insecure about his/her sexuality will make aggressive comments about gay people.

- The person who constantly suppresses his own tears will judge someone who openly cries for being overly dramatic or weak.

When you become aware of some of your projections, it is important that you don't start judging yourself for it. In fact, bringing awareness to your projections is one of the things that can really help you develop and improve the quality of your life.

All you have to do is become aware of the things you typically judge and become angry about in others and question whether you have those traits yourself. In this way your projections, and the people you dislike, can be some of your greatest teachers when it comes to improving yourself.

Here are some good questions to ask yourself:

- What am I constantly judging about others?

- What are some things that I absolutely can't stand in others?

- What things do I view as weakness in others?

- Is it possible that I have some of these same traits or perceived weaknesses and I just don't want to recognize them?

- Is it possible that I can't stand something about others because it is a reminder of some of my own unmet needs?

Always three fingers pointing back

The more you start accepting and approving of yourself, the more tolerance and compassion you are going to be able to feel for others. A common benefit of growing as a person is that you will stop noticing all the things that used to annoy you in others altogether.

Responsibility

Taking responsibility for your life is one of the most mature things you can do, and you will be amazed at how many irresponsible adults we have in our society.

Just because you are providing for yourself, have a place to live and a job, doesn't mean you are taking full responsibility for your life. Taking full responsibility for your life means that you stop blaming external situations and events and step up to the plate as the ultimate creator of your life experience.

Taking full responsibility is about realizing you are responsible for every single one of your emotions, thoughts, and actions. The actions, thoughts, and emotions you entertain repeatedly will eventually manifest into an external reality. If you are not happy with the current situation of your life, YOU are responsible.

No one is going to magically appear and solve all of your problems for you. There are two ways to take responsibility for your life: Either do something to change the situation you are unhappy about, or stop being unhappy about it.

There are so many people who are unhappy about their life situation and love to constantly whine about it. This is not taking responsibility.

If you are unhappy about your situation, it is time to get up and do something about it. If it is not causing you enough pain to do something about it, then stop your whining and accept that you have chosen this situation yourself.

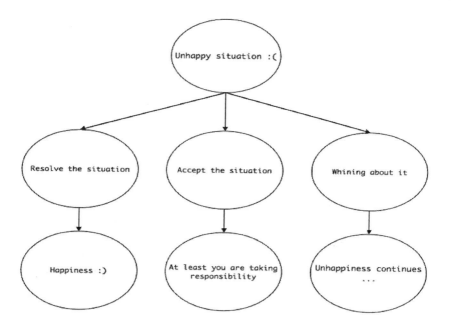

Examples of this:

- The husband who complains that his wife is no longer as attractive as she used to be.

- The wife who complains that her husband is verbally abusive or not romantic enough.

- The overweight person who complains about others' having a high metabolism, as if it is an explanation for why he/she is overweight.

- The person who whines about not having enough money for a vacation.

Take responsibility and realize that you are in the situation you are in because of you. You don't suddenly have debt, become overweight, or wake up to an unhappy relationship. These are all things that happen over time as a result of not taking responsibility for the things that needed to be done.

Take responsibility for the small things and they won't turn into great challenges. If you already have great challenges, then take responsibility now before they turn into gigantic challenges. Some people turn a blind eye to situations in their life that they absolutely know need fixing and think this is a good way to avoid pain.

Sure, you might temporarily avoid pain by not acknowledging something that needs fixing. However, over time, the challenge will become bigger and bigger, and suddenly you wake up and see that your spouse wants to leave you, that your child is addicted to drugs, that you owe massive amounts of money, that a lifelong abuse of food and alcohol has left you sick and weak, or that you are so depressed that you think about suicide.

No matter how big or small the challenges might seem, you need to take responsibility right NOW and start dealing with them.

The Magic Pill/Law of Attraction

A lot of people in today's society want guarantees for everything and won't take action unless they are absolutely sure they will get x and y results.

This is mainly caused by our being constantly bombarded with magic pills: "Buy this special abdominal machine and you will have a six-pack with just 3 minutes a day, buy our automatic software that makes you $300 a day while you sleep, take these secret Chinese herbal pills and you will lose 50 pounds in just 2 weeks," and so on.

Our mind has literally become programmed to laziness and wanting immediate results. For the same reason, taking consistent action and just having faith that you will eventually get what you want is not good enough for a lot of people.

It is actually one of the most common justifications people will use, "Well, I have gotten some results, but I don't think I can get the results I truly want, so there is no point in continuing."

Let's just burst the happy bubble of the magic pill society: **Worthwhile results are usually achieved through consistent action and discipline.**

I see a lot of people who completely stop taking action because they now "understand" the law of attraction and use it as a way to avoid taking responsibility in their life.

Sure, I definitely agree that it is powerful to believe that the universe will give you anything you want—but you have to actually plant a seed and water it before the flower will bloom.

Let's say you had a garden and wanted to grow some really beautiful flowers in order to win the annual gardening contest. Now imagine that this garden of yours has some of the most fertile soil ever. There are three different strategies you can follow in order to get exactly the flowers you want:

1. You can sit back and hope that the flowers will magically appear because you have such perfect growing conditions.

2. You can throw in a couple of seeds here and there and allow nature to work its magic.

3. You can throw in the maximum number of seeds possible in order to get the most benefit from the perfect growing conditions.

Of course, the best choice is step 3, where you plant the maximum number of seeds in order to get the most benefit from your fertile soil.

You need to focus on what you want to achieve and take the maximum degree of action towards it. The more action you take, the more seeds you plant. The more seeds you plant, the greater the chance you are going to get that perfect flower.

The great news is that you already have the most fertile soil ever and it is just waiting for you to start planting the seeds.

If you believe in the law of attraction, great, just make sure you also take the action you need to take. Once you have done everything you can with the resources you have, you can relax and let the higher powers work their magic. Just don't fall into the trap of never planting any seeds and wondering why the universe isn't bringing you all the things you desire.

> **"For every step you take toward God, God will take a hundred steps toward you."**
> **—Author unknown**

Responsibility for Yourself Versus Others

Even though most people don't take responsibility for themselves, they have no problem taking responsibility for others. They feel responsible for what someone said or did to them to such an extent that they carry around what happened in the past for years and even decades. Why does it matter what they said or did?

You are not responsible for the actions, emotions, or thoughts of others. It is a big enough job being responsible for yourself, why are you taking on an extra job?

A lot of people can be really peaceful and happy until the moment someone insults them or puts them down. By now you probably understand that what someone is expressing externally is only a continuation of what this person has to live with internally every single day of his or her life.

The Mind-Made Prison

If someone tries to insult me or put me down, I immediately get a view into the internal world of this person.

When you see where these people are coming from, the whole idea of "revenge" or "retaliation" seems stupid. Why would I ever want to kick someone who is already down and suffering?

These people can seem "powerful" or domineering, but if you just detach yourself from the situation and look at it without getting caught in the drama, you will see that their insults are just a sign of insecurity.

When you look at these people with compassion, you will see that they are in so much pain every single day that the only way they can deal with it is to try to project their pain onto others.

When someone insults you, just see it for what it is and then respond in any way you feel is best. Most people don't respond, they allow the other person's insult to reach their own internal insecurities and then react in a totally unconstructive way because they are "under attack." You can only be under attack if you allow something to affect you.

Let people think, say, or feel what they want, just as long as you are doing what you feel is the best thing for you to do. By taking responsibility for what others are doing, you are playing a losing game.

I am not saying that doing something that can make others happy is bad. I am not saying that you should go out and make people sad because you just don't care.

What I am saying is that you are not responsible for someone else's happiness or sadness. I am saying that you should do what YOU want to do, and as long as you are not physically harming anyone else or taking away their freedom, it is not any of your business what they feel, think, or do.

Examples:

- Let's say it is my mom's deepest wish for me to become a doctor and this has been one of her "goals" ever since I was a child. When I grow up I decide I don't want to become a doctor; I want to become an artist instead. Is it really my responsibility if my mom gets sad about my decision?

- Let's say you decide to break up with your boyfriend because you no longer feel the relationship is making you grow or is healthy. Is it really your responsibility if he decides to do drugs and get in fights as a way of reacting to the break-up?

- What if you apply to the same university as your friend and he gets rejected while you get accepted? Should you feel bad about getting accepted just because he didn't?

These might seem like obvious examples, but you probably also know that a lot of people are feeling emotional pain over similar events. I often get the same questions when talking about responsibility and therefore I want to make this really clear.

I am not asking you to be evil or to not have compassion for others. I see myself as a very giving person, and I always do my best to bring positivity, freshness, and joy to the lives of the people I affect. However, I will never do something that is detrimental to my own life because I feel responsible for someone else's happiness or sadness.

I respect the opinions of others, and if there is something I can do that will improve someone else's quality of life (without sacrificing my own), I will always do it.

But I will not change who I am or the expression of my truth because I suspect someone else is not going to like what I am saying. I will not show something I am not because I think that showing that trait will make someone else happy. For me, doing this is being inauthentic.

Everyone has the same talent and ability as you have. They choose the meanings they create, just like you do. For me, it seems awfully silly to sacrifice the quality of your own life because someone else hasn't realized their own God-given powers and wants to use their meaning-making skills to be unhappy.

Do your best to help people realize their inherent meaning-making skills, but never take responsibility for the unhappiness of someone else.

> **"I say NO to the demands of the**
> **world. I say YES to the longings**
> **of my own heart."**
> **—Jonathan Lockwood Huie**

Self-Esteem Versus Self-Confidence

There is a huge misunderstanding about confidence and self-esteem in our culture. This misunderstanding is one of the biggest reasons why people can feel worthless and constantly compare themselves to others.

Most people can't tell you the difference between self-esteem and self-confidence, and these two words are often used interchangeably in the media and society. If you think self-esteem and self-confidence are the same thing, you are making the game of life unnecessarily challenging.

I am now going to share with you my views on self-esteem and self-confidence. Once again, I have to mention that I can't prove that the beliefs I have about these concepts are true, and as you might have realized by now, absolute truth holds no importance for me.

All I care about is whether or not a given belief is improving the quality of my life. In this case, my views on self-esteem and self-confidence give me the freedom to constantly grow and express myself.

Self-esteem is your unconditional value as a human being. You have value simply because you are a human being and you are alive. Self-esteem has nothing to do with what you can or can't do, your level of achievement, or any other condition—your value as a human being is unconditional.

Self-confidence is based on your abilities and what you can do. Self-confidence is conditional, and the more or better you can do something, the more confidence you are going to have. We are all born without any self-confidence, simply because we can't do anything when we are born and we are completely dependent on our parents.

Self-esteem has to do with human being, and self-confidence has to do with human doing. Where most people go wrong is that they mistake their unconditional value as a human being for something that needs to be proven through achievement and doing.

If I look at a baby or a puppy, I am going to value them and feel compassion for them. I am going to acknowledge they are worth something, and I suspect most people would do the same. Can a baby or a puppy truly do anything for us? Do we value them because of what they can do, or does recognizing the simple fact that they are alive make them valuable?

Of course we can learn a lot from a baby or a puppy, but this is not what we value in them. We value their very being, and even though they don't yet have any capabilities, we recognize they are worth something without any conditions.

You are born with an unconditional worth, and you don't need to do anything to be worthy. You don't need to put up a certain façade to be worthy, and you don't need people to love you in order to be worthy. What experiences you went through have nothing to do with your worth.

You are already worthy because of the simple fact that you have life flowing through your body. I get a little emotional when I talk about this topic because it makes me sad that we sometimes don't realize our unconditional value. Sometimes we forget that every single human being, including ourselves, has an inherent value.

Sometimes we treat people (including ourselves) in a negative way just because we think they don't have as much value because they are poor, fat, ugly, or whatever. We are all valuable simply because we are here on Earth and the things we do and achieve don't make us any better or worse than any other human being. Everyone has his or her own purpose here on Earth, and therefore you can't judge whether someone is a "loser" or a "winner."

Realizing your inherent value as a human being will give you the freedom to just be you. So many people are forced into playing all sorts of roles in order to get validated by others and ultimately feel that they are worthy. You can skip all of the energy-draining activities you are currently doing in order to feel worthy and just know that you are worthy because you truly are.

Self-confidence is completely conditional and dependent on the abilities you have. How confident do you think Donald Trump would be if you put him on the Brazilian soccer team and asked him to play attacking forward? How confident would a world-class dancer be going head to head with Donald Trump in a business debate?

It is okay to have low self-confidence in an area of your life, in fact it is absolutely normal to have doubts about your skills in the beginning. However, you should never make the misinterpretation that your achievements and abilities have anything to do with your worth as a human being.

What you do, think, feel, and achieve is just an expression of what you are. Whether you feel depressed or happy, whether you are rich or poor, compassionate or selfish, good at what you do or not, has nothing to do with your worth as a human being.

This means you can go for all the things you want in life and fail miserably, as many times as you want, without affecting your true worth.

Except for death, nothing can ever take away the value you have as a human being. Death is the worst thing that can happen to you, and it is going to happen anyway. In fact, it is the only thing that is guaranteed in life. So, if the worst thing that can happen is already going to happen, then what is there to be afraid of?

Comparisons

Because most people see their worth in their capabilities and achievements, they naturally start comparing themselves with others. All comparison is competition, and you are competing to show that you are worth more than someone else. Isn't it ridiculous that we truly believe that having more paper with ink on it (money) is going to make us more valuable than someone else?

The act of comparing yourself-with someone else is the very first step to their becoming your enemy. A lot of people don't think comparing themselves with others is that drastic, but just imagine the following scenarios and feel how you would react:

- You get in an argument with your child and he tells you that X is a better parent than you.

- Your spouse tells you that the sex was a lot better in one of his/ her past relationships.

- Your spouse tells you that X is more attractive than you.

You see how quickly someone can become your enemy? It is not that you want to hurt this person; it's just that you build an often-suppressed resentment towards them for making you feel inferior.

The truth of the matter is that the person you are comparing yourself to didn't do anything. Your spouse, or whoever, said that someone else was better than you didn't do anything either. It is you who is making it into a big deal and making all sorts of comparisons, and who can blame you for doing this?

If you believe that your worth as a human being lies in your looks, capabilities, and achievements, you are going to feel severely threatened when someone is suddenly "better" than you.

Imagine what the pizza thinks when it watches the burger:

"Well, I have way more cheese than him and on top of that I have this delicious tomato sauce. But wait, he has that huge beef in there and a lot of lettuce! Well, that doesn't really matter because I look way bigger and I am eight delicious slices, while he is only one big clumsy piece. But wait . . . He has that delicious ketchup and homemade dressing that people really seem to like, and on top of that, his golden-brown sesame buns look really good! How can I ever compare to that? Oh, of course, how could I forget that I am topped with delicious pepperoni pieces? Go to hell, burger, I am way better than you!"

Meanwhile, the burger is doing the same thing and sizing itself up against the pizza.

This is exactly what we are constantly doing in our lives, we are in a constant mode of comparing ourselves with others and it drains a lot of our energy. We compete with others to prove that we are better, and we often forget what we really want in the heat of trying to "win."

I see people working 80-hour work weeks because they are stuck in beating their competitors. In reality, they would rather come second or third and spend more time with their family.

I am not saying there is anything wrong with working hard. I am saying it is important to be aware of why you are doing something so you don't spend your whole life chasing the pot of gold at the end of the rainbow. Are you doing it to become a better you, or are you doing it to become better than someone else?

If you are in it for the actual journey and you are enjoying yourself along the way, great. Just don't expect to reach a final destination where you are going to finally be content because you are now better than others.

There is always going to be someone who is more attractive, wealthier, more intelligent, what have you. It is a game you can't win, and by playing in a way where you can be better than someone, you are also playing in a way where you can be worse.

Everything is constantly shifting, and if your worth is based on external conditions, your sense of worth is constantly going to go up and down.

Isn't this how most people live their lives?

We feel powerful and confident when things are going our way and weak and pathetic when we are knocked down by life.

There is no big race in life and there are no enemies. You are only competing against yourself, and everything else is just lessons to be learned. All of your "enemies" are just teaching you lessons that you can use to further develop yourself. Do you think this is a powerful meaning to live by? You bet it is!

"Fear of competition in your business? Good news, there is none! Nobody is you, can do what you do, in just the way you do it."
—Brenda Johima

There are lessons to be learned in every second of our existence. Go into nature and look at rivers, mountains, butterflies, and ants. Stay at home and look at your cat or dog or go to work and learn from the boss whom you dislike so much.

Go out into the world and look at how people are acting, listen to music, watch a movie, read a book, think back on every single experience you have had in your life, and there is always a lesson to be learned.

The only question is whether or not you are aware enough to pick up the lessons you are being handed.

One of my favorite activities is to ask myself what I can learn from a given situation and then come up with an answer through honest reflection (I know, I am a self-development nerd!).

You can either blame an event or reflect upon the things life throws at you and learn whatever you can.

Sometimes I talk with people who are absolutely fed up with their lives. Even though they logically know that there is always something to learn, they just feel like they have been hit with too much tragedy at once.

When I look at what is going on in some of these people's lives, I think, "Wow, they are absolutely right. That is a whole lot of challenges they have been presented with at once." Maybe you are currently in such a situation too.

I completely appreciate that when life hits you hard, it can be difficult to view those challenges in terms of learning something and moving forward.

I really believe that everything happens for a reason. I always tell these people that if God (or whatever higher force you believe in) has presented them with so many challenges at once, it must be because He not only believes they can handle it, He absolutely expects them to step up to the plate and prove to themselves what kind of unlocked potential they possess.

Besides, there really is no other choice than moving forward, is there? You might as well give it your all, learn as much as you can, and move forward as the new and improved version of you!

I recently read an absolutely remarkable story about a Dutch woman called Monique van der Vorst. At the young age of 13, Monique lost the use of one of her legs due to an ankle surgery that went completely wrong.

Even though Monique was partially paralyzed, she didn't let this stop her. She took up hand-cycling and won six European and three world championship titles!

In 2008, she was hit by a car, and the injuries to her spinal cord were so severe that she became completely paralyzed from the waist down. Do you think she let this stop her? Later that year she competed in the Beijing Paralympic games and won two silver medals!

Here comes the part that really puts tears in my eyes. In 2011, Monique was in the shape of her life and was training very hard for the 2012 Paralympics in London.

Things didn't go exactly as planned, however, and Monique was involved in an accident with another cyclist. Her body went into a spasm and suddenly she started to feel a tingling in her feet.

A couple of months later, she was walking fully again and she is now dreaming of riding in the 2016 Olympics! This is the power of learning something from everything life throws at you and just continuing to move forward.

If you are in the right state of mind, some of the biggest perceived tragedies in your life can also be some of the most influential ones in terms of getting a higher quality of life.

Not learning from the lessons you get

I used to know a guy who had a big heart and was very giving to others. However, he also happened to have a really bad temper, especially when he was driving.

He was always yelling at other drivers, and he really was a poster boy for road rage. It got to the point where I didn't want to sit in the car with him anymore, as I knew there was an accident waiting to happen.

What was very interesting to me was that this man was having the same experience over and over again in his life. Every time he got in the car he was almost guaranteed to get angry with another driver, and he failed to see that it was his own fault.

It was always the other person who didn't know how to drive, and he was so stuck in the blame game that he didn't see the lesson at hand.

I just know that the moment this man stops blaming others, takes responsibility and learns the lesson at hand, the "jackasses," as he calls them, will stop appearing and everyone will magically become good drivers.

I know this because I have seen it in my own life and the lives of others, time after time.

We have already talked about this in great detail: What you believe in is also what you focus on, and what you focus on is constantly going to get reinforced because you keep finding evidence for it. This will lead to the same life lesson over and over again, until you finally get the lesson and stop the cycle.

The moment you get what you were supposed to learn, you will have improved your life quality a little and can move towards the next lesson with a little more peace of mind.

Some examples from my own life:

I used to get in arguments with people all the time, and it would give me a lot of emotional pain. I finally learned the lesson when I realized that there is nothing for me to defend, as everyone has his or her own truth anyway.

Quite naturally, I stopped getting into arguments with people, and I realized that I had always had the power to stop these arguments. The only reason I was constantly getting into arguments was because I "chose" to, or rather, my beliefs chose to do so on my behalf.

I also used to play the role of someone who didn't need anybody and could do it all on his own. This made me feel lonely because I missed out on a lot of opportunities where I could have connected with people instead of pretending that I didn't care.

I finally learned the lesson when I realized the only reason I was doing this was because I was afraid of trying to connect with someone and then getting rejected. It was not because people had nothing to offer, as I had justified this behavior in my mind.

Immediately I started connecting with others on a much deeper level, and I understood that everyone has something unique to offer.

These situations were recurring events that kept coming up in my life until I learned the lessons that were being presented. This is the process of life, and I have no doubt in my mind that there are thousands of lessons for me to learn that I am not even aware of right now.

There are so many lessons to be learned for each of us that it is never too late, or too early, to get started. Each lesson learned will get you closer to your true potential and further improve the quality of your life.

You can only start learning your specific lessons once you let go of the blame mentality and take responsibility.

Transformation Exercise

Really take the time to look at what recurring experiences you are having and if there is an underlying lesson you are missing.

As you can see, the concepts I have shared with you in this chapter can make or break your life. By becoming aware of them and stopping them from affecting your life negatively, you will move towards transformation.

If you implement the things I have discussed in this chapter into your life, you are guaranteed to soar to new heights.

> **"Everyone thinks of changing the world, but no one thinks of changing himself"**
> —**Leo Tolstoy**

CHAPTER 6
Time to Question Things

This chapter is all about getting deeply personal. Before we get into the actual questioning, I want to share with you some of the things that can hold you back when it comes to growing and developing.

The fact of the matter is, you are NOT going to develop if you view self-improvement and spirituality as just interesting hobbies.

This is a trap the majority of people who are into "improving" themselves get caught in at some point during their development, and I know this trap intimately since I have been in it myself.

We read something because it is "motivational," and it gives us a surge of determination until we crash again a couple of days later. We listen to all kinds of self-improvement programs and really feel that we are getting somewhere because we are studying so vigorously.

We go to seminars where we jump, dance, and scream, only to return to our old beliefs when the weekend is over. We get all sorts of certificates and master degrees with the sole goal of validating that we really are changing and developing.

We even start spotting other people's perceived faults and feel really special for being able to see what others are doing "wrong."

This is NOT what the path of self-improvement is about. Self-improvement can ONLY happen by going inside. Because there is so much focus on the external aspects, like seminars, private coaching, and reading many books, in the self-improvement industry, it is very easy to get caught in the trap of using all of those things to avoid looking inside, where the real change always takes place.

Studying is good, but real wisdom comes from using that knowledge in your life and becoming aware of the underlying beliefs that are running your life.

If you are interested in self-improvement, not just the image or feeling of growth, then make sure you do the exercises in this chapter properly.

Your mind doesn't want you to look inside because this means risking that you will become aware of some of your "protective" programs.

In most cases, your mind just wants the feeling of growth and not the actual growth. In most cases, your mind would rather stick to the beliefs it has viewed as true for so many years. Even if some of your beliefs are causing you suffering and pain, your mind might view it as even more pain to have to change them.

Your mind will do anything to preserve the imaginary picture it has created of who you are.

Your mind will try to rush you to move to the next chapter and come up with all sorts of justifications for why it is currently not the best time to do the exercises. It will start comparing what you read in this book to other methods in order to figure out what is "true." This is just another means of keeping the attention focused outward and thus avoiding self-inquiry.

Your mind will be overly critical and closed when it sees the word "exercise." It will start daydreaming and taking your focus away from looking inward.

It will say, "Ahh, I already know these methods, there is no need to do them again"; this particular defense mechanism is one a lot of people who are into self-improvement use.

Knowing on an intellectual level is NOT the same as knowing on an emotional level.

Your mind will tell you, "This won't work, so there is no need to even try." Don't believe these stories. All I ask of you is to put away all of your stories when going through this chapter and really give the exercises a sincere try. If the exercises don't work, you can always go back to your old beliefs again and you will not have lost anything.

However, there is a lot to gain. The self-inquiry you get to do in this chapter has the potential to help you realize some of your limiting beliefs and thereby give you more freedom and joy.

If you are in a rush right now, I suggest you wait until another time when you can take the time and really get to the bottom of your beliefs. This chapter is probably going to take some time to get through if you are being really thorough with the questions, which you should be if you want the maximum benefit.

View the process as a game where you are going to uncover as many of your limiting beliefs as possible.

At this point, it's a really good idea to go back to chapter 4 and re-read the part on self-inquiry and questioning before moving to the exploration of your beliefs. In fact, I suggest you do that right now, before moving on.

In some places I have asked you to define a given term, such as success. It is important that you don't just use the dictionary definition of the word; I want you to use your definition. While anger is a means of power to one person, it can be a means of weakness to another. Your definitions alone will give you a lot of knowledge about your beliefs.

I want you to view each single question as an opportunity to go really deeply into the structures of your psyche. This means that if you answer a question and you feel that digging deeper into your answer is going to give you some valuable information, you should definitely go for it.

Question your answers with "Why?", "Is this absolutely true?", "Is this who I really am?", and use all the other questioning tools you learned in the self-inquiry chapter.

There are two reasons why you should write down all of your answers: It will make the answers easier to process, and you will be able to come back in a few months or years and see how you have changed. You are more likely to have transformative realizations if you write your answers with as many details as you can.

Go with the flow and see where the self-exploration takes you. Remember, there is no rush, and last but not least, enjoy yourself!

> **"A man travels the world over**
> **in search of what he needs and**
> **returns home to find it."**
> **—George Moore**

Life Quiz

Self-Image

What type of person do I see myself as?

What type of person do others see me as? Is this congruent with how I see myself? If not, why?

Do people like me for who I really am or for a façade I put up?

What things do I really like about myself? Why do I like these traits?

What traits or reactions do I dislike about myself? Why do I dislike these traits?

What are my major strengths and weaknesses? How would it change my life if I focused on using my strengths more and balancing out my weaknesses?

What are some of the areas of my life where I am really confident? What areas am I less confident in? How are the areas that I am less confident in affecting my life? How are the areas that I am confident in affecting my life?

What are some of the accomplishments I am really proud of? What feelings did these accomplishments give me?

What are some things I have done and experienced that I am not proud or ashamed of? Why?

What period of my life do I like the most, and what period do I dislike the most? Why?

What things and people do I try to avoid in life? Why do I avoid these particular people and events?

What secondary benefits am I getting from avoiding these people and events?

What things or people do I typically move toward? What is it about these people and events that I really like? Am I absolutely sure that my assumptions about these people and events are true? What secondary benefits am I getting from moving towards these people and events?

What is one of the most important goals for me right now? Why is the attainment of this goal important?

Do I have an easy time expressing my emotions and thoughts? Why is it easy or hard for me to express myself?

Do I have any habits that are really productive in terms of the quality of my life?

Do I have any habits that are destructive to the quality of my life? What secondary benefits am I getting from these habits? Are these secondary benefits worth the negative effects these habits have in my life?

Do I approve of myself 100%? Why or why not?

What things do I want people to remember me for when I die? Why?

Do I believe that my worth is unconditional or that it is based on external conditions? Why?

How big an impact does my current self-image have in my life on a scale from 1 to 10?

Are my beliefs in this area improving the quality of my life?

What new empowering beliefs in this area can really improve the quality of my life?

Money

What is my definition of and association to money? (Not the dictionary definition, your definition.) Is this definition constructive to the quality of my life?

What beliefs about money did I learn from my parents or social circle? (Money doesn't grow on trees, all rich people are greedy, you will only get one or two chances to make big money, making money is hard, you have to work 24/7 to become a millionaire, etc.)

Am I absolutely sure that all the beliefs I learned about money are true?

Do I feel negative or positive emotions about money? Why?

What level of income do I want?

How much money do I feel I deserve to earn a year? Why do I choose this specific amount and not something higher or lower?

What does it mean to me if I don't make as much money as I feel I deserve? Why?

What do I love to spend money on? Why?

What do I dislike spending money on? Why?

What are some of the financial habits I have that are decreasing the quality of my life? How are they decreasing the quality of my life?

What are some of the financial habits I have that are increasing the quality of my life? How are they improving the quality of my life?

How important is money to me on a scale from 1 to 10?

Are my beliefs in this area improving the quality of my life?

What new empowering beliefs in this area can really improve the quality of my life?

Attractiveness

What is my definition of being attractive? Is this definition constructive to the quality of my life?

Am I in control of when I feel attractive, or is the external world in control? Why?

How attractive do I give myself permission to feel?

How important is feeling attractive to me on a scale from 1 to 10? Are my beliefs in this area improving the quality of my life?

What new empowering beliefs in this area can really improve the quality of my life?

Success

How do I define success? Is this what I truly feel or something I chose because that is how society has defined success?

Do I give myself credit for the success I have already achieved? Why or why not?

What level of success do I feel I deserve in life? Why this specific level?

How important is success to me on a scale from 1 to 10?

Are my beliefs in this area improving the quality of my life?

What new empowering beliefs in this area can really improve the quality of my life?

Love

What is my definition of love?

Are there some particular things that make me feel like I am really loved? Does my partner know that I would like him/her to do these things for me?

What are some of the things I do that give me a feeling of sharing my love with others? Do I need to do more of these things?

What are some of the beliefs I have about love? (Love will eventually fizzle out, true love is hard to find, there is no such thing as a soul mate, etc.)

Do I assume my spouse has the same definition of love as I do?

What level of love do I deserve to receive from myself? Why?

What level of love do I deserve to receive from others? Why?

How important are love and connection to me on a scale from 1 to 10?

Are my beliefs in this area improving the quality of my life?

What new empowering beliefs in this area can really improve the quality of my life?

Trust

What is my definition of trust?

How trustworthy a person do I perceive myself to be? Why?

Do I have permission to trust others?

How important is trust to me on a scale from 1 to 10?

Are my beliefs in this area improving the quality of my life?

What new empowering beliefs in this area can really improve the quality of my life?

Anger

How do I define anger?

Do I usually suppress or express my anger? Why?

Do I have permission to feel angry?

What are some of my beliefs about anger? (Anger is bad, others don't like angry people, anger means you are out of control, etc.)

Are these beliefs improving the quality of my life?

How important is expressing or suppressing my anger to me on a scale from 1 to 10?

Are my beliefs in this area improving the quality of my life?

What new empowering beliefs in this area can really improve the quality of my life?

Gratitude

What is my definition of gratitude?

Is this definition improving the quality of my life?

How often do I feel grateful in life?

Would it improve the quality of my life to feel grateful more often?

How important is being grateful to me on a scale from 1 to 10?

Are my beliefs in this area improving the quality of my life?

What new empowering beliefs in this area can really improve the quality of my life?

Failure

How do I define failure?

How many times do I have to miss my target before I will call it quits and accept that I have failed? Why?

What beliefs do I have about failure? (Failure means getting ridiculed by others, if you fail more than three times you should stop, successful people don't fail, etc.)

What do I think others will think of me if I fail?

How important is avoiding failure to me on a scale from 1 to 10?

Are my beliefs about failure improving the quality of my life?

What new empowering beliefs in this area can really improve the quality of my life?

Honesty

What is my definition of honesty?

Do I view myself as someone who is honest?

Do I feel people are generally honest? Why or why not?

What are my beliefs about honesty? (Honesty is the only way, people will take advantage of you if you are too honest, honesty only works with other honest people, etc.)

How do I think honest people are perceived in society? Why?

How important is honesty to me on a scale from 1 to 10?

Are my beliefs about honesty improving the quality of my life?

What new empowering beliefs in this area can really improve the quality of my life?

Sex

What does sex mean to me? Is it a means of connecting? Is it a necessary part of a relationship?

How much do I enjoy sex on a scale from 1 to 10? Why not more?

What beliefs do I have about sex? (If you have sex with many people you are cheap, you have to know someone for X amount of time before you have sex with them, sex is sinful, sex is completely natural, etc.)

What does great sex mean to me?

Does my partner know what I view as great sex and vice versa?

Do I feel negative or positive emotions in regard to sex? Or both? Why?

Do I have a hard time expressing my sexuality?

How do I think others view sex?

How important is sex to me on a scale from 1 to 10?

Are these beliefs decreasing or increasing the quality of my life?

What new empowering beliefs in this area can really improve the quality of my life?

Happiness

What is my definition of happiness?

Do I have permission to be completely happy right now? Why or why not?

What are my beliefs about happiness? (People who are happy all the time are lunatics, happiness is overrated, I can't be happy until I achieve my goals, if you are happy you lose all motivation, etc.)

Am I in control of my happiness. or is it determined mostly by the external world?

Do I express my happiness to others?

Are there any negative sides to being happy?

How important is happiness to me on a scale from 1 to 10?

Are my beliefs in this area improving the quality of my life?

What new empowering beliefs in this area can really improve the quality of my life?

Friendship

How do I define friendship?

How do I know if someone is really my friend? Is it based on how long I have known them, the connection we share, or something entirely different? Why?

Do I have a few friends or many? Why?

What are some of the favorite things I enjoy doing with friends? Why?

What beliefs do I have about friendship? (True friends are hard to find, if you become too close to someone they will hurt you, friendship is not that important, etc.)

Do I view myself as a good friend? Why or why not?

What changes could I make to my attitude in order to become a better friend than I currently am?

What do I value about friendship? Do my friends know what I value in a friendship and do I know what they value?

How important is friendship to me on a scale from 1 to 10?

Are my beliefs in this area improving the quality of my life?

What new empowering beliefs in this area can really improve the quality of my life?

Spirituality

How do I define spirituality?

How spiritual do I perceive myself to be?

Do I believe in God? Why or why not?

What do I do in order to connect with my spiritual side?

What are my beliefs about spirituality? (Waste of time, only something New Age people do, an absolutely necessary part of life, etc.)

How important is spirituality to me on a scale from 1 to 10?

Are my beliefs in this area improving the quality of my life?

What new empowering beliefs in this area can really improve the quality of my life?

Guilt

In what situations in life do I feel guilty? Why do I feel guilty in these situations?

Does it improve the quality of my life when I feel guilty about things?

Do I have things from the past that I am still feeling guilty about?

How important is it for me to avoid the feeling of guilt on a scale from 1 to 10?

What new empowering beliefs in this area can really improve the quality of my life?

Self-Improvement

What is my definition of self-improvement?

Do I typically feel I am growing, or do I feel I am not really getting anywhere? Why?

What are some of my beliefs about self-improvement? (Self-improvement just hides the underlying problems, if you are not growing you are dying, self-improvement is an ongoing process, etc.)

What do I assume my social circle thinks about concepts like growth and self-improvement?

How important is it for me to feel like I am growing on a scale from 1 to 10?

Are my beliefs in this area improving the quality of my life?

What new empowering beliefs in this area can really improve the quality of my life?

Inner Peace

How do I define inner peace?

Do I believe inner peace is something only yogis get to experience, or is inner peace an emotion everyone can feel on a consistent basis?

How often do I feel inner peace? Do I want to feel inner peace on a more consistent basis?

Can I just generate the feeling of inner peace, or does everything in my surroundings have to be perfect before I can feel peaceful?

Do I see myself as someone who has inner peace?

Do I have any negative associations to the concept of inner peace?

How important is inner peace to me on a scale from 1 to 10?

Are my beliefs in this area improving the quality of my life?

What new empowering beliefs in this area can really improve the quality of my life?

Responsibility

How do I define responsibility?

Do I take complete responsibility for my life? Why or why not?

Do I take responsibility for the thoughts, feelings, and actions of others? Why or why not?

How important is taking responsibility for my own life to me on a scale from 1 to 10?

Are my beliefs in this area improving the quality of my life?

What new empowering beliefs in this area can really improve the quality of my life?

Time

Do I feel like there is an abundance of time or a lack of time? Why?

What age do I expect to attain? Why this particular age?

What beliefs do I have about time? (Time just flies, the older you get the faster time will go, without time everything would be chaos, etc.)

Do I typically use the concept of time in a constructive way, or does it give me stress?

What change in attitude would I have to make in order to have a better relationship with time?'

Are my beliefs in this area improving the quality of my life?

What new empowering beliefs in this area can really improve the quality of my life?

Career

What is my definition of career?

Why did I first become employed at the place I am currently working?

Is there anything I love about my work? Why?

Is there anything I dislike about my work? Why?

What sort of work would I be doing if I could choose anything in the world? Why?

What has stopped me from pursuing my dream job until now (if anything)?

What beliefs do I have about career and work? (Starting your own business is very risky, true security comes from working for someone else, no one likes their job so you just have to deal with whatever puts food on the table, etc.)

How important is a career to me on a scale from 1 to 10?

Are my beliefs in this area improving the quality of my life?

What new empowering beliefs in this area can really improve the quality of my life?

Health

What is my definition of health?

Am I happy with my current level of health? Why or why not?

What beliefs do I have about health? (Whether you are healthy or not is based mostly on your genetics, life is too short to worry about being healthy, my health can be sacrificed as long as I have a successful career, etc.)

What are the top challenges for me when it comes to becoming healthier? Why?

What shift in attitude would help me overcome these challenges?

How important is health to me on a scale from 1 to 10?

Are my beliefs in this area improving the quality of my life?

What new empowering beliefs in this area can really improve the quality of my life?'

Relationships

What is my definition of a relationship?

Am I happy in my current relationship? Why or why not?

What are the challenges in my current relationship? Are these challenges something I can live with? Why or why not?

What would I like to change about my spouse? Why?

Could I be happy even if my spouse didn't change the aspects about them that I don't like?

What did I like about my spouse when I first met him/her and what do I like about him/her now?

What beliefs do I have about relationships? (You can't be happy if you are not in a relationship, only weird people are single, a passionate love isn't important as long as you are just content with each other, etc.)

How important is the area of relationships to me on a scale from 1 to 10?

Are my beliefs in this area improving the quality of my life?

What new empowering beliefs in this area can really improve the quality of my life?

Fear

What are my beliefs about fear? (Fear just means that I am getting closer to the truth, if I am afraid of something it is okay to not do it, fear always means danger, etc.)

What are a couple of things I really fear in my life right now? What would it mean to me if those things happened? Why?

Do I use fear as an excuse not to move forward with the things I truly want in life?

Do I believe fear is always an indication of danger?

How important is it to me to avoid the things I fear in life on a scale from 1 to 10?

Are my beliefs in this area improving the quality of my life?

What new empowering beliefs in this area can really improve the quality of my life?

Food

What are my beliefs about food? (Food is medicine, food is just designed to fuel the body, food is a source of pleasure, food gives me comfort, etc.)

How big of an impact could it make on my life if I changed some of my current eating habits?

Are my beliefs in this area improving the quality of my life?

What new empowering beliefs in this area can really improve the quality of my life?

People

What are my beliefs about people? (They all just want something from me, they are out to scam me, people are all inherently good, etc.)

Do I usually mingle with strangers or try to stay away from them? Why?

Do I typically view myself as better than, worse than, or equal to others? Why?

What is the worst thing that can happen when interacting with a stranger? Why?

What is the best outcome that could happen when interacting with a stranger? Why?

What change in attitude would improve the general quality of my interactions with the people I meet? How would this attitude improve the quality of my interactions?

Are my beliefs in this area improving the quality of my life?

What new empowering beliefs in this area can really improve the quality of my life?

It is mentally tough for most people to do this kind of self-exploration, as a lot of stuff they weren't aware of suddenly comes up. I want you to make a mental note of the most important things you learned about yourself and create an action plan for how you can start changing the things that would create the biggest improvement in the quality of your life. The belief changer and negative evidence finder are two tools that can really help you with doing this.

I asked you to grade each area of your life on a scale from 1 to 10 in importance. This grading tells you a lot about the things you find important in life. It is a good idea to evaluate whether some of the things that are actually important to you have been underprioritized in your life.

Most people are usually surprised to find that areas that are extremely important to them have been neglected because they weren't really aware of how much they valued those areas.

If you really feel like moving on to the next chapter, then by all means go ahead. However, I recommend that you take a break and take some time to reflect on what you can take away from this self-exploration and how some of your insights can improve the quality of your life.

**"Knowing yourself is the
beginning of all wisdom."**
—Aristotle

CHAPTER 7
Going Your Own Way

By now you have started seeing some of the beliefs that are holding you back. You have also learned how you can use the power of meaning to transform the quality of your life.

These teachings alone will continue to have an effect in your life for many years to come simply because there are always more limiting beliefs to unravel and more personal freedom to claim.

Success is not a destination, and there is no magical place to get to. The more you work at it, the more rewards you are going to see.

When it comes to implementation of what has been learned, a lot of people like to set up extreme plans of action where they suddenly try to completely redesign their life overnight. If this approach works (and has worked for you earlier), then by all means go for it.

However, it is my observation that most people will have greater success if they start out small and build momentum as they move forward.

We have all attempted to implement thousands of new things in our lives all at once. A typical example of this is our New

Year's resolutions. We wake up on the first of January and start a new diet, fitness regimen, meditation plan, and completely new self-development program. What usually happens is that we feel overwhelmed after a couple of days and end up quitting.

This is not a long-term strategy for most people, and therefore it is not how I suggest you continue.

I am an avid follower of the kaizen philosophy of making small incremental changes that add up over time. These changes are not going to take huge amounts of work, but once you get the momentum going, the returns will be great.

It is all about getting the momentum going for you. Even though it might seem like a little work in the beginning, you have to see this process as an investment in yourself and understand that the longer you stick with it, the easier it is going to get.

Let me give you a very simple example of how something small can build in momentum over time.

In this example we are going to assume that the number of calories you are currently consuming is just enough to keep your weight stable, meaning that you are neither losing nor gaining weight.

Imagine that your life was really stressful for a couple of weeks and you started drinking a 12-ounce can of soda every day during your break, to cool down and get some energy.

However, when your life settled back to normal, you were so in the habit of drinking this 12-ounce can of soda every day that you just continued doing so.

Now most people don't think that a single can of soda each day will make a huge difference to the quality of their life, but let's take a look at the numbers. One pound of fat is equal to just about 3,500 calories, and a 12-ounce can of soda contains 155 calories.

This means that after 1 month of continuing this habit, you have consumed 4,650 additional calories and you have gained just about 1.3 pounds. This seems pretty insignificant, doesn't it? Let's do a fast-forward in time and look a little further into the future.

When you reach the 6-month mark of drinking this one can of soda every day, you have consumed just about 28,000 calories and gained 8 pounds of fat. The results are still pretty small, but you can now see and feel that you have gained a little bit of fat around your belly and thighs.

Since it is a pretty normal routine to drink a can of soda a day, we are now going to look at what this does after 24 months.

If you don't change anything else in your life other than drinking a can of soda a day over the next 2 years, you are looking at 32 pounds of extra weight. Bear in mind that this is just one can of soda and that most people have a variety of these "small" snacks throughout the day.

If you are just looking at 32 pounds of extra fat, you are still missing the larger picture. Gaining an additional 32 pounds of fat is going to affect a wide range of things in your life. It is probably going to affect your sex life, confidence, energy level, health, and relationships.

These are, in turn, going to affect your finances, career, and so on. When these different areas of your life are affected, you are going to feel even more stressed out, and the chances that you will overeat even more increase. This starts a new vicious cycle, and the decline in life quality continues even faster.

Now you could also remove 155 calories a day from your current diet. If this is the only thing you do, you are going to lose 32 pounds of fat over the next 24 months without doing ANYTHING other than drinking a can of soda less than you currently do.

This is going to affect a lot of other areas of your life positively and lead to your making even more positive changes. This is the power of making small incremental changes that add up over time.

> **"Do not fear going slowly; only**
> **fear standing still."**
> **—Chinese proverb**

I am going to suggest that you implement one new activity into your life and let it build momentum. This activity will allow you to start trusting your inner knowing and move forward in life with additional courage and passion.

We will get to this particular activity later in this chapter. First you need to fully understand why you need to trust your inner knowing.

There is no one else here on planet Earth that has had the same experiences, thoughts, emotions, struggles, and success that you have had up to this point. As a meaning maker, the meanings you create are unique, and this gives you a unique perspective on life.

This is why the path of self-exploration is ultimately one that you have to take alone. Sure, you can have friends who support you or join a spiritual community. However, you are the only person who knows exactly what you need and when you need it.

Over the past couple of years I have realized that as a teacher I have two primary tasks.

The first is to be completely present with the client.

The second is to guide them in the direction of uncovering their limiting beliefs and to help them realize what it is they already know deep down inside.

I view my work as being a connection expert who simply helps someone reconnect with the inner knowing they already possess. Once you teach someone to start trusting their inner knowing, you have given them the greatest gift you can ever give as a teacher.

Most of us know exactly what we need and want to do in our lives, and in most cases, not knowing isn't the challenge at hand. The real challenge is usually not having enough trust and belief in ourselves to actually go out and get started.

Most people become programmed to ignore their inner knowing because they associate it with risk and potential failure. Your soul is always talking to you and guiding you; the question is whether you trust its higher wisdom or not.

Even when it comes to self-improvement, we will feel more inclined to seek out the most popular methods simply because that is what everyone else is doing.

This is fine, and completely natural to begin with, but in order to fully grow into the potential that is unique to you, there comes a time when you need to surrender to your intuition and follow it wherever it takes you.

This can be very scary because most people have been programmed to do the opposite and follow the herd their entire lives. They have been taught that the most stable and secure way in life is to simply do what everyone else is doing.

However, the fact of the matter is that following the herd will in most cases just give you an average quality of life, and that's if you're lucky.

You really need to set yourself free from the herd mentality and start disconnecting from what everyone else is doing and do what you want to do instead.

In a world where the majority of people are asleep, it is simply irresponsible to look to others for instructions on how to live your life. Sure, you should listen to as many people as you can, but in the end it is up to you and you alone to make the decisions that are best for you.

Just look around you with awareness and you will understand why. Most people are living in a state of worry and fear with some joyous moments sprinkled in once in a while.

Most people aren't happy with their lives and are constantly wondering "What if?"

Most people don't feel or look healthy, and most people don't have the financial freedom to do the things they have always wanted to do.

Most people think their clothes, car, or job defines them. Talk about setting yourself up for unhappiness! Most people don't have the freedom of expression to just let go and celebrate life with a crazy dance! Some people don't even see what there is to celebrate!

My observation is that we live in a society where ideas like superficiality, materialism, and image have become more important than human connection, happiness, and joy.

If you want the highest quality of life possible, you can't afford to be brainwashed by society, your social circle, family, social institutions, media, me, or any other person claiming to know what is best for you.

Only you know what is truly best for you.

NO authority or expert in the world knows you better than you know yourself. Therefore, it is important that you start appreciating your own input on how to live your life.

Take in all the different perspectives and then have the courage to listen to your inner knowing and make the decision that seems right at that moment.

Sure, you will make mistakes, fail, take the wrong turn, and so on, but as long as you are doing the best you possibly can, what more can you expect of yourself?

My definition of living up to your potential is that you always strive to take the route that seems the best possible option at any given moment.

> **"The greater danger for most**
> **of us lies not in setting our aim**
> **too high and falling short; but**
> **in setting our aim too low, and**
> **achieving our mark."**
> **—Leonardo Da Vinci**

If you are not failing, it doesn't mean you are just THAT good, it simply means you have grown stagnant and are not pushing yourself anymore. Never failing simply means you are playing it a little too safe.

Why is it important to listen to your inner knowing? Because it will bring you a level of joy, peace, and happiness that you could never imagine. Because it will allow you to earn a living doing what you love.

Because you will enjoy what you are doing so much that you will gain an incredible level of expertise within your given craft and because the moment you do so, you are no longer doing something just in order to get it done.

By following your intuition, you will become an artist who puts their very being into what they are doing and will continue to do so until they create a life that is a proud representation of everything they stand for.

Your inner knowing doesn't care about whether someone is going to laugh at you or judge you; all it cares about is being who you are meant to be. All it cares about is embracing the person you were born to be.

Who were you born to be?

We are all artists. If you don't give yourself permission to share your gifts and talents with the world, you are never going to be truly fulfilled. You will always live with some sort of regret. It will be a waste of your potential if you don't share with other people your unique gifts to the world.

Be a nurturer, an artist, a businessman, a wonderful friend, a great father, a fantastic lover, a spiritual teacher, or an architect; it doesn't matter what you do as long as you listen to what your gut is telling you and do what you are meant to do.

Doing this will make sense on the very deepest level of your being because it is so much easier to be who you ARE and always have been instead of trying to live up to a superficial picture you picked up along the way.

Now, how in the world are we going to start connecting to our inner knowing? Actually, you have already begun the process by having the courage to question some of your old beliefs about the world and being open-minded enough to explore.

The three-step process I am now going to share with you is quite simple, but it is important that you follow through and commit to it.

The Three-Step Process to Reconnecting with Your Inner Knowing

The first step lies in bringing awareness into your life. You need to recognize the things that are currently working in your life and the ones that are no longer serving you.

We have already started this step and have looked at a lot of our beliefs about the world. I still recommend that you take a look and see if you can find any additional "dead habits" and beliefs that are currently holding you back.

By dead habits, I am referring to anything in your life you continue doing solely because you have been doing it for so long.

Typical examples of these "dead habits" are:

- Jobs that stopped being interesting years ago and you are just sticking with because it is a lot more comfortable than going out and risking failure in the pursuit of what you really want to do.

- Beliefs and habits that, even though comfortable, are lowering the quality of your life.

- Staying in a relationship you see no future in simply because it is easier to do so.

- Religious or spiritual practices that are no longer making sense to you but you continue pursuing because you fear the consequences of not doing so.

There is a story about a man called Bill that is a great example of this. Bill really loved to eat sausages, and luckily his wife Janine had no problem making him sausages with her homemade chili sauce whenever he felt like it.

Bill really appreciated the fact that his wife took care of him and made him his favorite dish whenever he wanted it. However, even though he was grateful, something had annoyed him for quite a while.

What was getting a little on his nerves was the fact that Janine always cut the sausages in half before putting them in the frying pan. He had remarked about this a couple of times, but he didn't want to seem like he was ungrateful, so he eventually let it go.

One day, after a long day at work, he finally decided to complain to Janine about her cutting the sausages. He asked why she didn't just put them in the frying pan without cutting them first.

When Janine realized he wasn't just joking around, she told him she had just learned it this way from her mom. This surprised Bill a little, and even Janine realized it was a little silly that she had never questioned why her mom did it in this way.

Their confusion quickly turned into curiosity. Bill decided to call Janine's mom to ask why she did this. Janine watched Bill's face carefully as he talked with her mom, and she really didn't like the smirk on Bill's face when he put down the phone. "What was her reason?" Janine asked inquisitively. "Well, she didn't know. She just said she had always cut the sausages in half before putting them in the frying pan because it was what her mom had always done," Bill replied.

Now Janine really wanted to know the reasoning behind this tradition even more than Bill, so, she picked up the phone and called her grandmother, Mae.

After talking with her for a few minutes, she finally asked her why she always cut the sausages in half before putting them in the frying pan. She started laughing uncontrollably when she got the answer.

Bill eagerly waited for Janine to say goodbye to her grandmother and tell him the reason. When she finally put down the phone, she said, "Honey, I won't cut the sausages in half anymore. You can have them any way you like." Bill felt a surge of satisfaction that decreased a little when he realized he still didn't know the answer to the sausage enigma, "Why did she do it?" he asked.

Janine blushed and replied, "Grandma Mae told me they couldn't afford the large frying pans back in the day, and because they only had a small one, she was always forced to cut the sausages in half. She also said she didn't like doing this because her husband always complained about how sausages tasted better when they weren't cut in half!"

Are there any habits in your life that are decreasing the quality of your life but you continue engaging in them simply because you are so used to them?

Listen to your inner knowing (the little voice in the back of your mind that is usually ignored) and you will immediately know which areas of your life have become unproductive habits that need to be changed.

> **"You have to leave the city of your comfort and go into the wilderness of your intuition. What you'll discover will be wonderful. What you'll discover is yourself."**
> **—Alan Alda**

Step two of the process consists of rediscovering or discovering the things that you really enjoy doing. Most of these activities usually go all the way back to your childhood, although you may have discovered some of them in your adult life.

Do you remember when you were a kid and you drew pictures? You didn't draw those pictures in order to be done with them, did you? You drew them because you loved every second of doing so and you felt so proud when you went around showing your finished piece of art to everyone. This is what you need to get back to!

Some people immediately know what these activities are for them. For others, it can be a little harder to get in touch with this aspect of themselves.

In order to make this part of the process as easy as possible, you can use the following guidelines:

- It doesn't matter how significant or insignificant the thing(s) you find seem.

- Don't think about it too deeply. This is not a thinking matter, it is more about feeling and intuitively connecting with the things you really love to do.

- Look at some of the things you already know you enjoy doing and feel what it is about that activity that you really enjoy. See if there are other activities that can give you this same feeling.

- Example: If you really love being a lawyer because you like playing around with words and formulating points in just the right way, you might also enjoy writing poetry.

- Ask yourself what you would be doing if there were no limits in your life and you could do anything you wanted to.

Whether you get a big or small list of things doesn't really matter; what's important is that you have at least one thing you would enjoy doing that you are not already doing in your life.

Once you find one activity you would really enjoy doing, it is time to move on to step 3.

The third step of this process is the "doing" part. Before your mind starts going on a rant about how it doesn't like the doing part of exercises, you need to remember that what you are going to do is something you actually enjoy doing.

I recommend you take just one thing and get started on it. It doesn't matter whether you are committing 5 minutes or 8 hours a day to doing what you have chosen, and I would even suggest that you start out small. What matters is that you actually get started, no matter how big or small an impact you think this given activity is going to have on your life.

Trust me, doing this will have a huge effect on your life. It will slowly but surely start shifting your attitude throughout your day. The shift isn't caused so much by the actual activity you are doing, but more by the fact that you are actually taking the time to nurture and heal yourself. No matter how stressful your day might seem, you know that you have a time where you can just let go and be you.

Everybody needs nurturing and healing. It doesn't matter if you are a hotshot salesman, a loving mom, a schoolteacher, a born leader, or a monk, we all need to take some time off to connect with who we are. It is crucial that we take responsibility for our own healing and nurturing and put aside the time to take care of ourselves.

If you are not happy, you can never bring true happiness to the lives of others. Whenever someone asks me about the concept of self-love, I tell them that self-love simply means putting your own oxygen mask on first instead of trying to help others and then fainting.

If you are not taking care of yourself first, you are not thinking long-term and you are an accident waiting to happen.

Taking time for yourself is not a bonus that you can afford only once or twice a year; it is an essential part of functioning fully.

How much is it going to benefit your loved ones and the people you are responsible for if you suddenly have serious physical or mental problems?

How much value are you offering your family when you let the frustration from your work affect them?

How much love can you really give to others when you are in constant regret over not following your dreams?

How can you truly give advice to someone when you are ignoring all the advice you yourself are getting from within?

You absolutely need to give the one activity you choose an honest shot and start implementing it into your daily life. At least give it your best shot before deciding whether it is a waste of time or not.

The activity you have chosen is designed to get you to take the time to nurture and love yourself.

With time and consistency, this small activity is going to build your self-love. The reason for this is simple: Only people who feel worthy of their own attention and love will give themselves permission to do something that would give them those emotions.

How often do you give yourself the attention and love you really deserve?

Transformation Exercise

Stand in front of a mirror, look at yourself with complete appreciation, and say "I love YOU, thank you for everything you do for me. I know that deep down you have nothing but the best intentions for me, and I appreciate everything you do, even when things don't go exactly as I had planned."

Most people in life are not going to have any qualms about putting you down and projecting their own insecurities onto you; this is okay because we are not responsible for what others do or think.

However, it is kind of silly when you put yourself down and don't give yourself the positive attention and nurturing you need. Is it really necessary for you to put yourself down when there are so many volunteers out there who are going to do it anyway?

> **"You, yourself, as much as**
> **anybody in the entire universe,**
> **deserve your love and affection."**
> **—Buddha**

The more you get into the activity you have chosen, the more connected you are going to be to your inner knowing. With time, you will build the courage needed to follow your inner guidance on some of the bigger dreams and aspirations you have.

It will teach you to start trusting your inner knowing more and recognizing whether situations in life are serving you or not.

Last but not least, you are going to be so much more playful in your everyday life. We walk around so serious about everything in our lives and because we have done it for so long, we think doing this is absolutely normal and the only way to live.

What are we so serious about? Death and poverty? Is this what is so serious? Well, without death and poverty, we wouldn't be able to experience life and wealth. We live in a world of duality, and the rainy days are just as important as the sunny ones.

Life isn't as serious as most people perceive it to be. You can choose to see life as a big game and play your way through it or to view it as something serious where you just have to get through unscathed. The irony is that somehow it is always the people who try to go through life unscathed that are hit the hardest.

Common obstacles to starting your chosen activity

Sometimes I see a few stumbling blocks when it comes to listening more to your inner knowing and doing the things you have always wanted to do. I am going to briefly address these and hopefully this will allow you to get off to a flying start.

Some people start coming up with various excuses, for example:

- I don't have time to play around like this.

- This is all just some New Age stuff.

- I don't have enough energy to sit and connect to my inner self; I need to put food on the table.

- What are people going to think of me if I start doing this? It would seem pretty weird.

- I can't let go of the things I have been doing for so long.

By now, you already know the solution to these and any other objections you may have. Start questioning them and see whether they are improving the quality of your life or not.

Among the biggest obstacles I see when it comes to going your own way and doing the things you really love are people's social circles.

Most people get a huge surprise when they realize that those who love them the most can also be the ones who are going to resist the positive changes they make the most.

Most of the people around you don't really want you to change either "negatively" or "positively." This is not because there is a huge conspiracy and everyone is out to get you; it is simply how the unaware mind functions.

When people's beliefs are controlling them, and not the other way around, they will do anything in their power to get their external reality to fit their beliefs, even if this means resisting the idea that things and people in their surroundings are constantly changing.

How others are going to react to the changes you make is going to depend greatly on their values and their upbringing. The key is to understand that it really doesn't matter how people are going to react to the changes that you make, as long as they feel right for you.

You are here to make yourself happy first and everybody else second. Just realizing that people are going to resist almost any change (including yours) can give you some reassurance in tough times when your mind starts feeding you destructive beliefs such as:

- Maybe I am really taking this "taking care of myself" a little too far.

- Is it really that important to express myself?

- I just want others to be happy, even if it is at the expense of my own happiness.

- Maybe they are right, I am a grown-up and it is stupid for me to take some time off to just do activities that I love and cherish.

It is important to stick to your guns and stand by the changes you have chosen to make when people start questioning you.

This doesn't mean you should get mad and yell, "You are just unaware and all you are doing is resisting the change I am making in order to uphold your own beliefs of the world."

I know it can seem tempting at times, but there is just something paradoxical about someone pointing fingers and yelling at others while calling them unaware!

It doesn't mean you should start questioning whether they really love you, and it doesn't mean you should get paranoid and feel that there is a conspiracy intended to hold you back. There is in fact a conspiracy; the conspiracy is not against you, however, but *for* you. This conspiracy has the sole purpose of making you grow as much as possible and allowing you to build additional courage in your life. View all the resistance people give you as giving you the chance to reinforce the new and improved you.

See all the resistance people give you as an expression of love and understand that they are only resisting because they fear you might not love them as much if you change and improve.

This is the power of meaning, and it is what I have been preaching throughout this book. I am handing over the mantle to you and asking you to start using this power to ensure you will stick to the activity you have chosen.

It might seem tough to face resistance in the beginning, but if you stick to your guns it is only a matter of time before people accept that you are in fact a "transformed" person, and this becomes part of their new beliefs about you.

> **"There is nothing like returning**
> **to a place that remains**
> **unchanged to find the ways in**
> **which you yourself have altered."**
> **—Nelson Mandela**

To sum up:

- It is a lot more effective to make one small change that you stick to than 10 big changes that you give up on.

- In order to be truly fulfilled, and to be able to bring the maximum amount of joy and passion to your own life and the lives of others, you need to listen to the inner guidance you are getting.

- One way to slowly start trusting your inner wisdom is to take one activity that you would really enjoy doing and implement it in your everyday life. This is just a starting point, and as you start trusting that your inner knowing is guiding you towards the highest quality of life, you will know what steps to take next.

- Make sure you at least give it a shot before you decide whether just doing one simple activity on a daily basis can make a huge difference in your life or not. Remember the example about a single can of soda a day?

- Doing small things on a consistent basis can have an immense and transformative power.

- Understand that the resistance of others is completely natural and just an additional opportunity to grow and express your true self.

Last but not least, I want you to have fun with this. This is not a task, it is an opportunity to do something that you actually love and have missed doing, either knowingly or unknowingly, for a very long time.

This is an opportunity to connect with the child within you. Don't ever forget the child you still are, the child who loves to play around and get lost in something fun for hours!

You need to embrace this part of you and nourish it, even if it is for just 5 minutes a day. Your inner child is longing for fun, don't deny him the chance to play in a world that is, in reality, just a huge theme park, a theme park just begging you to let go of your fear and jump on the biggest and baddest ride and see where it takes you.

If you stick with it, you might even realize you are not the person you have pretended to be for all this time and that you have been selling yourself short.

There is a beautiful Zen story about a lion that grew up among sheep. A herd of sheep found this lion when it was just a cub, and because they didn't know what type of animal it was, they decided to take care of it. However, as the lion grew up, the sheep started realizing he was a very different animal than they were.

They could see that he was taller than the biggest ram and that his color was that of the sun rather than the clouds. Even though this lion had a broad, muscular jaw filled with razor-sharp teeth, it learned to go along with the rest of the herd and live on a diet of grass. Because this lion had never known any other life than that of the sheep, it even bleated like a sheep.

The Mind-Made Prison

One day, a ferocious wild lion attacked the flock of sheep, and as it was trying to determine which sheep it wanted to eat, it suddenly noticed the other lion in the middle of the flock. At first the wild lion became a little apprehensive and got ready to fight the other lion for the territory and the food. However, after a few seconds, the wild lion realized that the lion it was preparing to fight actually thought it was a sheep.

The wild lion was flabbergasted, to say the least, and he decided to drag the "sheep-lion" down to the river. On the way there, the sheep-lion whimpered and begged the wild lion to spare its life.

When they finally got to the riverside, the wild lion forced the sheep-lion to look at its reflection in the water. When the sheep-lion saw that it resembled the wild beast that was going to kill him, it got scared and tried to back away from the water.

The wild lion grabbed him and pushed him forward to see his reflection once again. When the sheep-lion saw its reflection for the second time, the other lion looked at him with compassion and said: "Don't run away from who you are. You may have grown up with a herd of sheep, but you always have been and always will be a magnificent lion. You are courageous, independent, and a lot more powerful than you can ever imagine."

In that life-changing moment, the sheep-lion realized its true power, and he expressed his liberation by letting out the first roar of his life.

CHAPTER 8
Where Do You Go from Here?

So, where do you go from here and how can you start incorporating the information I have provided into your life?

The implementation of the information can be incredibly simple if you want it to be. The most successful people in all arenas of life are those who just stick to the basics and do the simple stuff over and over again until they get to where they want to be.

It doesn't matter if you are studying to be a monk or a business mogul like Warren Buffet.

The monk gets up every morning, does some work around the Monastery, and then gets on with his studies and meditation.

Warren Buffet gets up every day, does whatever it is he has to do, and then sits down and studies the market for up to 8 hours.

There is no advanced formula for peace, success, or happiness.

They are all just the result of sticking to the basics and becoming better and better through practice. The cool thing about sticking to the basics is that often you will start seeing results very quickly and the results will keep improving the more you stick with it.

The Mind-Made Prison

Likewise, the solution to liberating yourself from the mind-made prison is quite simple. Pick one or two concepts that you really liked in this book and start focusing on them in your everyday life.

Make it a game to find these concepts in as many situations as you can and constantly search for areas where they can improve the quality of your life. When you want some variety, come back and pick one or two other concepts and start playing around with them instead.

Nothing in life is really that serious, and therefore I don't want you to make a big deal out of your self-improvement. Be focused, but remember that it is all just play and it is important to have as much fun as you can with the things you do.

Even though I can be quick to talk about how things have gone wrong with our society, people, and the world in general, I absolutely love having the experience of being a human.

I believe we have come a very long way as a species, and things are a lot better than they could have been when you consider all the factors involved. I believe all humans are inherently good and that sometimes we just take the wrong turn without really knowing why.

Therefore, I don't want you to walk away from this book seeing the flaws of society and people and start looking down on them in order to "grow." More separation from each other is the last thing we need.

We have so many fantastic and incredible qualities that are not coming through because of all our insecurities. By including yourself and others instead of excluding them, you are creating an avenue for true expression to come through.

As I am writing this last chapter, it has also become time for me to leave Turkey, where I initially started writing this book and where I have lived for the last 3 months.

I have been living in an area where there are a couple of homeless dogs. It has been fascinating to me how these dogs eat almost 8 to 10 times a day because everyone is so eager to give them their leftovers.

When people approach these dogs to feed them, I sometimes catch a glimpse of something in the eyes of these people who are usually shy and hold themselves back.

I catch a glimpse of compassion and affection that is so deep, I get tears in my eyes. I get so emotional because this is the same inner divinity we usually don't express to others because of our insecurities.

I absolutely know that if people can have this level of compassion for a couple of homeless dogs, there are no limits to the level of love we can have for our own species once we stop believing our limiting beliefs and insecurities.

I believe all of our problems here on Earth are caused by our insecurities as human beings. If you start allowing just 1% more of your true self to shine through, you have done a great service not only to yourself, but also to this planet and the rest of humanity.

> **"Your task is not to seek for love,**
> **but merely to seek and find all**
> **the barriers within yourself that**
> **you have built against it."**
> **—Jalal ad-Din Rumi**

I want you to start becoming softer in your everyday life. Don't take things so seriously and give yourself permission to look like a fool sometimes. Start expressing who you are to the world, don't save the expression of your innate perfection for when you meet a dog or a baby that is going to accept you no matter what.

EXPRESS what you are and allow people to reject it if that is what they want to do. Just make sure to at least express that beautiful soul of yours. Embrace the vulnerability of putting yourself completely out there and just letting whatever happens, happen.

Have more deep feelings of intimacy and moments where you are laughing so hard you have tears in your eyes and you just can't stop yourself.

Embrace the nervousness of having to do something for the first time and not knowing how it is going to go. Seize the opportunity to go out and meet some complete stranger and get a brief look into their perspective on life!

Go for what you truly want in life with no reservations, just because it is the thing that feels right to YOU. Whatever you do, don't play it safe! Life itself is a once- in-a-lifetime opportunity. It is such a pity to just settle and never get to experience the magnificent potential that is deeply rooted in your very being.

Don't play by someone else's rules in order to make them happy or content! This is YOUR shot at the incredible miracle of life, and you have to play by the rules that feel right for you and not the rules that others are trying to impose on you.

Life is so simple. You are born, you have a lot of different experiences, and then you die.

If you constantly try to stand in the way of the dance, it will not feel right. Let go and allow the dance of life to unfold in the exact manner that it should.

Mateo Tabatabai

Let go, knowing that nothing can ever hurt what you are at the very core and that everything here on this planet is just another experience for you to go through.

Let go and let God.

With deep love and compassion,
Mateo

P.S. I would really appreciate it if you would review my book on Amazon.com, Amazon.co.uk, or Goodreads. If you do review my book, please send me an email at mateo@mateo-t.com so I can thank you personally.

References

Luck Study, http://www.damninteresting.com/
you-make-your-own-luck/ Luck Study by professor Richard
Wiseman

http://www.createthefuture.com/past_quotes.htm

http://www.best-self-help-sites.com/beliefs-quotes.html

http://www.imdb.com/title/tt0112883/

http://www.wisdomquotes.com/topics/awareness/index2.html

http://ucs'r.ucsf.edu/index.php/hrupdate/update200202.htm
lottery winners and injury

Barbara De Angelis quote is from *Women's Journal*, 8 August
1998

http://www.inspirational-quotes-short-funny-stuff.com/
belief-quotes. html

http://www.nytimes.com/2010/06/06/books/review/Bloom-t.html

http://jessiekaitlyn.wordpress.com/quotes/

http://creativenudge.com/
quotes-on-competition-and-creativity-inbusiness/

http://www.huffingtonpost.com/2011/11/27/paralympian-joins-
procyc_0_n_1113723.html

http://www.wisdomquotes.com/topics/acceptance/

http://graciousliving.typepad.com/the_write_event/2007/08/
thereticular-a.html

About the Author

Mateo Tabatabai has dedicated himself to the transformation of his own life and the lives of his fellow humans. He is a Global Management Engineer and has spent the last 7 years traveling the world in a quest to hone his skills. Mateo is now adding to the knowledge obtained from world masters in self-improvement and therapy by formally working towards a master's degree in psychology.

Visit http://www.mateo-t.com for private sessions, video products and free gifts.

Made in the USA
Middletown, DE
31 January 2016